A Victorian Courtship

A Victorian Courtship

The Story of
Beatrice Potter and Sidney Webb

Jeanne MacKenzie

New York
Oxford University Press
1979

First published in Great Britain by
Weidenfeld and Nicolson
91 Clapham High Street   London sw4

First American edition, 1979
Oxford University Press, New York

ISBN 0–19–520166–3
Printed in Great Britain

For Hope and George Spater
with affection

Contents

Illustrations

Acknowledgements

I AM grateful to the British Library of Political and Economic Science for permission to use copyright material from the Passfield Papers and to the Society of Authors on behalf of the estate of George Bernard Shaw. I would also like to thank Norman MacKenzie for his help and for material drawn from his *Letters of Sidney and Beatrice Webb*, published by Cambridge University Press in 1978.

A Grown-Up Young Lady

'SO ALL in all I am to be the old maid of the family,' Beatrice
Potter wrote to her sister Mary in April 1888 on the engagement of their youngest sister, twenty-three-year-old Rosie.
On the face of things this was a surprising remark since Beatrice was a handsome and well-endowed woman of thirty.
She had a keen and intelligent face, a beautiful voice, deep
brown eyes and thick brown hair coiled smartly in a bun;
and besides, as she said, she was one of 'the fashionable Miss
Potters who live in grand houses and beautiful gardens and
marry enormously wealthy men'. A smart match seemed the
natural destiny for the nine daughters of Richard Potter, a
rich railway promoter and timber merchant with a country
house in Gloucestershire and a fashionable London mansion
close to Kensington Gardens.

Once Rosie was married, Beatrice would be the only one
of the sisters left at home. Lallie, the eldest of the girls, born
in 1845, had married long ago in 1867. Her husband was
Richard Holt, one of a ship-owning family of Unitarian
Liberals in Liverpool. Kate had married late; she was in her
middle thirties when, in 1883, she became the wife of the
up-and-coming Liberal MP Leonard Courtney. Mary, one of
the family beauties, was the wife of Arthur Playne, a mill-
owning squire in the Stroud valley in Gloucestershire. Georgina, tall and handsome with a proud unbending nature, had

married the banker Daniel Meinertzhagen in 1873. Blanche, the loveliest and most troubled of all the sisters, was married to a distinguished surgeon named William Harrison Cripps; and the delicate but lively Theresa had married his younger brother Alfred Cripps, already making a mark as a lawyer and a rising Conservative politician. In 1880 the plump and intelligent Margaret, four years older than Beatrice, married Henry Hobhouse, a country gentleman from the well-known Liberal family, and went to live on his family estate at Hadspen in Somerset.

Richard Potter was pleased to see his daughters so well settled in life; Beatrice, indeed, felt that he had played his part in the match-making. 'It was he', she wrote, 'who married seven headstrong self-willed women to men he thoroughly approved and considered suitable; and prevented, without forbidding, all other marriages.' Only Rosie, with her wilful and rather artistic temperament, had chosen an unsatisfactory husband – an ailing and ineffective lawyer named Dyson Williams. Richard Potter naturally hoped that Beatrice would do as well as the older daughters. 'A woman is happier married,' he told her as she passed the customary age for a Victorian girl to be settled. 'I should like to see my little Bee married to a good strong fellow.' All the same, in the years that he had been a widower she had become his companion and hostess, and he was accustomed to her presence in the house. He could count on her.

Beatrice accepted this convenient role, which matched her image of herself as a woman devoted to the life of useful work which was so often the mark of a spinster; and she was already making something of a name for herself as an investigator of social problems. Though she was not altogether reconciled to her lot of private domesticity and public service, after years of heartache she had learnt to be philosophic about it. 'Life to me is becoming every day more interesting,' she told Mary in 1888, 'and more impersonal – but at times one feels weary and lonely. I suppose one must pay one's penny and take one's choice – and on the whole I am satisfied with my existence.'

The life of the Potter daughters certainly seemed enviably comfortable and lively. The family history was a typically Victorian story of success against adversity, of public spirit combined with material prosperity, of religious piety fused with intellectual curiosity. Richard Potter had grown up in a family of Nonconformists in Lancashire. His father was a man of considerable initiative and energy who made money in the Manchester cotton trade and sat as the Radical MP for Wigan in the first Reform Parliament after 1832; his uncle, also a Radical, sat for Manchester; and the two brothers were founders of the great Liberal newspaper, the *Manchester Guardian*. His mother was a dark-eyed fiery-natured woman of gypsy appearance who spoke Hebrew and had a delusion that it was her mission to lead the Jews back to Jerusalem. She was so highly strung that at times she was unbalanced, and she spent long periods away in an asylum. Richard inherited some of his mother's unconventional restless spirit but for the most part he was like his father, affectionate and open-hearted, a practical man full of enterprise if lacking refinement and polish. After graduating from University College, London, which his father had helped to establish, he amused himself in London society and after being called to the Bar he took the grand tour of Europe.

While he was in Rome he met Laurencina Heyworth and they were married in 1844. Her family background was very like that of her husband. Her father, Lawrence Heyworth, had risen to be a wealthy merchant in Liverpool and in 1847 he became MP for Derby. He had married his servant, who was 'a bonny one to look at', but she came from a family with a strong streak of melancholy; she had died young leaving a family of sons and one daughter. It was, inevitably, a household dominated by men and Laurencina, the solitary girl, had even been named after her father. She was a woman of striking appearance with considerable intellectual gifts and ambitions who had grown up in a political atmosphere with her father and brothers and she enjoyed arguing with the distinguished men who came to the house. She had been brought up to be a scholar as well as a gentlewoman, and as the wife of Richard Potter she looked forward to a life of learned leisure.

Richard Potter, heir to a substantial fortune, had been discouraged from earning a living at the Bar and the young couple settled down in Herefordshire to live on his income. All went well until he lost the greater part of his capital in a bank failure in 1848. He then had to make a new start and his father-in-law, Lawrence Heyworth, one of the promoters of the Victorian railway boom, helped him by making him a director of the enterprising Great Western Railway; by 1863 Richard Potter's energy and enterprise had made him chairman of the board. He had also gone into partnership with a schoolfriend who had a timber business at Gloucester and he did well out of supplying huts to the French and British armies in the Crimean War. From this position of vantage, said Beatrice, 'my father became a capitalist at large'. Before long he was a man of considerable wealth and influence with investments in Europe and America – for ten years he was President of the Grand Trunk Railway of Canada – and he was always willing to take a risk on a new venture.

These manifold commitments took Richard Potter away from home a great deal but he was a strong family man. 'His own comfort,' said Beatrice, 'his own inclinations were unconsidered before the happiness of his wife and the welfare of his children.' He was, indeed, so devoted to his wife, and so dependent on her, that this uncritical attitude affected his judgement and Beatrice considered her mother to be his 'evil genius'. It was Laurencina's restless ambition that spurred him on: it was her imagination that stimulated his passions. 'Was it the necessity of "managing" his wife's temper (since from love of her he dared not defy her) that made him an intensely reserved man?' she asked herself. 'He told all; he left all untold.'

In some respects the normal parental roles were reversed. Beatrice said that it was her father rather than her mother who was 'the light and warmth of the home', admiring and encouraging his daughters while Laurencina seemed to hold herself emotionally aloof from them. Beatrice certainly did not find her 'motherly'. Laurencina, an orphaned and only daughter, had never had an example to follow in the arts of motherhood or felt confidence in herself as a woman; in a family of boys she had learned instead to admire masculine virtues and the distractions of childbearing intensified her resentment at Victorian domesticity. The strain of melancholy in her mother's family, the Akeds of Bacup, came out in Laurencina's introspection and her fits of depression. Even her pleasures – she occupied herself with philosophical questions, studied foreign grammars and capped her interest in economics by translating some essays by her friend Michel Chevalier – were scarcely the thing to cheer a woman who was house-bound for much of her life. She also wrote a novel, *Laura Gay*, but the reviews were not encouraging. Her ambitions were all intellectual ones, and the conflict between undeveloped feeling and introspection made Laurencina a restless and nervy woman. 'Mother gets anxious as usual whenever there is a possibility of so doing,' Theresa noticed; 'it seems to me that some sort of anxiety is quite indispensable to her existence and when there is none in reality she feels bound to imagine it'. And such anxiety underlay the tactless and dogmatic manner in which Laurencina advanced her views – a characteristic which her daughters imitated to the point where the Potter girls were said to be too decided in their opinions and too forceful in expressing them. They carried frankness to excess.

It was an odd household in its human relationships, but outwardly the Potters conformed to the conventional lifestyle of well-to-do Victorians with an informed interest in the world. The family home, which Richard Potter leased from Lord Sherborne in 1853, was Standish House in Gloucestershire. This substantial stucco residence with a lake in front of it stood among beech woods at the foot of the Cotswold ridge and looked across the broad valley of the Severn estuary to the Malvern hills and the Forest of Dean on the western skyline. It was here that Beatrice was born on 22 January 1858. For all its imposing grandeur Beatrice never cared for Standish. She thought it was more like an institution than a home, run as it was with impersonal efficiency.

Beatrice, for good reason, felt her mother's emotional frigidity more severely than her older sisters. The austere comment – 'My strength much impaired by having little Beatrice, my 8th daughter' – was the way in which Laurencina described her birth in her diary. Her mother really longed for a son and when Beatrice was four her wish was realized. Little 'Dicky' was the Potter's only son and he absorbed all Laurencina's affections while he lived, and all her grief when the two-year-old boy died on Christmas Day 1864. He was, said Beatrice, the 'crowning joy and devastating sorrow' of her mother's life and after his death Laurencina Potter withdrew into herself more and more and gave herself up to her intellectual pursuits. Creeping up in the shadow of her baby brother's birth and death Beatrice felt neither ill-treated nor oppressed – merely ignored. 'My childhood was not on the whole a happy one,' she concluded when she looked back on it in later life; 'ill-health and starved affection, and the mental disorders which spring from these, ill-temper and resentment, marred it; and its loneliness was absolute.' Beatrice tried hard to understand her mother and she grieved silently at the gulf between them. 'What is this feeling between mother and me?' she asked herself in 1873. 'It is a kind of feeling of dislike and distrust which I believe is mutual. And yet it ought not to be! She has always been the kindest and best of mothers, though in her manners she is not over affectionate. She is such a curious character

I can't make her out. She is sometimes such a kind good affectionate mother full of wise judgment and affectionate advice and at other times the spoilt child comes out strong in her.'

Although the older sisters were friendly and interested they had their own concerns of love and marriage; Beatrice found it hard to make friendships with them and they did little to offset the lack of motherly attention. For relief from the formal routines of family life Beatrice turned to the informal intimacy of the servants' quarters. She would take refuge in the laundry and curl up among the sheets and table-cloths, or she would sit on the ironing-board and chat to the maids about her intention to become a nun. Sometimes she would retreat to the hay loft or the shrubbery to build castles in the air and brood over the want of love around her. And in this large household of children, servants and governesses she found a warm-hearted and protective friend in Martha Jackson – 'Dada' as the family called her – a distant poor relation of Laurencina Potter who had been her companion since her marriage and used her sympathy and sense of humour to mother all the girls in turn. Beatrice saw her as a saint – 'the one and only saint I ever knew'. But Martha Jackson could not completely fill the gap left by Laurencina's neglect; and in her loneliness Beatrice copied her mother and withdrew into herself. At the age of fifteen she started to keep a diary. 'I must pour my poor crooked thoughts into somebody's heart,' she said, 'even if it be my own.'

While the Potters were among the most respected and prosperous families in Gloucestershire they played little part in the settled life of the county. For them the quiet routine of country life was constantly interrupted. They were always on the move: 'the restless spirit of big enterprise dominated our home life', said Beatrice. And there were any number of visitors – relatives, business associates, American railway presidents and Scandinavian timber growers, intellectuals of all schools of thought, religious, scientific and literary. There was, said Beatrice, 'a miscellaneous crowd who came into and went out of our lives, rapidly and unexpectedly'.

One frequent visitor was Herbert Spencer, a civil engineer turned philosopher, who had made an immense reputation with books on the theory of social evolution which extolled the popular individualism of the age. He had met the Potters in 1845 soon after their marriage – 'the most admirable pair I have ever seen', he declared. He had been struck with Laurencina's 'unusually graceful and refined manner', her zeal in the anti-Corn Law agitation for freer trade and cheaper food, when she distributed tracts and argued for the cause. Laurencina, Spencer said, was 'scarcely less argumentative than I was'. He found Richard Potter 'the most lovable being I have yet seen', and was impressed by the 'beauty of his disposition'. Spencer was not an easy man, nor even very likeable, for he was crotchety and self-centred, increasingly hypochondriacal and pedantic; but he was a kindly man and devoted to the Potters – he would go fishing with Richard Potter, who did not care much for his theories, and he would engage in philosophic discussion with Laurencina. And as their children grew up he took an interest in them and in their education. He was a bachelor and he enjoyed the company of these lively young girls; he broke the schoolroom routine by taking them for country walks to look for plants and fossils. While they teased him for his fussy spinsterish ways they also respected him. Kate, on holiday with him in Egypt in 1879, wrote to her mother to say that 'Mr Spencer has tumbled into his usual place of being a half interesting and half tiresome irrational being to be occasionally fought and generally managed and smoothed down.'

Spencer treated Beatrice (or 'Beebo' as she was often called) as a particular favourite, responding to her intellectual curiosity and encouraging her in her studies. He told her that she was a 'born metaphysician', reminding him of George Eliot whom he regarded as the 'most admirable woman he had ever met – mentally'. Beatrice, neglected as she felt herself to be, naturally responded to his attention. As she grew older she remained fond of him, even though she became more critical of his ideas and his way of life. 'There is something pathetic in the isolation of his mind,' she wrote, 'a sort of spider-like existence: sitting alone in the centre of his theoretical web, catching facts and weaving them again into theory.' Even so she was enormously influenced by his philosophy and by his self-denying dedication to his work, by his respect for factual evidence and by his insistence that new scientific ideas which were undermining religious faith could also be applied to the analysis of society. It was Spencer who brought to the Potter house such prominent scientists as Francis Galton, Sir Joseph Hooker, John Tyndall and T.H. Huxley, Darwin's outspoken champion.

Darwin's *Origin of Species* was published the year after Beatrice was born and she grew up in the shadow of the controversy it evoked. Exposed to an intellectual atmosphere at an early age, Beatrice was keenly aware of the problems of religion, philosophy and science in such a household. 'We lived,' she said, 'in a perpetual state of ferment.' There were more practical interests too: as her brothers-in-law, more or less evenly divided between Liberal and Conservative sympathies, were actively engaged in politics in the heyday of the struggle between Gladstone and Disraeli, she was well aware of the issues of the day. And as her father shared his business worries with all the family (and pamphlets explaining new economic theories would appear in her mother's boudoir) she realized that questions of trade, wages and worklessness were important even if she could not understand them. It was a peculiarly open-minded family for its day. Everything from 'sexual perversion to the rates of exchange' was frankly discussed and the Potter girls were encouraged to browse freely in the excellent family collection or to borrow from the London Library and Mudie's. If a book was unavailable or the libraries had found it too improper to stock, Richard Potter would respond to his children's curiosity with the words: 'Buy it, my dear.' He took the view that 'a nice-minded girl can read anything'.

Deprived of emotional comfort, increasingly lonely and wilfully independent, Beatrice turned to intellectual comfort: under Spencer's ponderous guidance she tackled equally ponderous tomes and wrote about them at serious length in her diary. She was seized by a feverish intensity to discover 'the truth'. While she found all the talk and ideas stimulating she also found them confusing, for she had little formal education to absorb and discipline her curiosity. Laurencina thought her the least intelligent of her children and for the most part Beatrice was left to pick up what she could from the governesses and tutors who were employed to teach the older girls. At the age of sixteen, when she was sent, for a time, to Stirling House, a smart finishing school at Bournemouth, she did not take easily to being taught; for she had already acquired the habit of working on her own and, at the same time, a sense of intellectual condescension, though it troubled her, kept her apart from her school-fellows. 'I must above everything endeavour not to think myself superior to the other inmates of Stirling House because I have been brought out more by circumstance and encouraged to reason on subjects which other girls have mostly been told to take on faith.' Beatrice had grown up with the belief that 'everyone, aided by a few elementary text-books, could be his own philosopher and scientist'.

From 1863 the rhythms of London society guided the movements of family life. In April each year Richard Potter took the family up to London for the Season, and for some time 47 Princes Gate served as their London home. When Beatrice was old enough she joined her sisters in the customary social pursuits of girls of their class – horse-riding in Rotten Row, dancing, giving parties, flirting with eligible young men looking for marriage partners, visiting the club at Hurlingham and Ascot races. For a time there was a fad for charades and theatricals. In May 1873 Theresa wrote to

Beatrice in great excitement about the rehearsals for *She Stoops to Conquer*, and telling her of the expected audience: 'Mrs Charles Dickens will be there and one of her daughters.' And a few months later Beatrice was writing of her pleasure in the Season. 'I enjoyed it immensely,' she wrote. 'The Theatricals – the Dance. Oh how I did enjoy that. It was the first dance I have ever been at as a grown-up young lady.'

Beatrice, like her sisters, loved the whirl of pleasure, yet for all of them there were pangs of high-mindedness and guilt about such worldly indulgences. In 1875, for instance, the pain of rejecting unsuitable proposals drove Kate into a life of independence. She decided to leave home and take up social work with Octavia Hill, a determined philanthropist who had turned from a blighted love affair to a dedicated campaign to clear the slums in the East End of London. Kate's decision only confirmed Beatrice's feeling that it was vanity and self-indulgence that drew her to the social attractions of the capital. By the time she was eighteen she decided that she did not wish to 'come out'. She wanted something more – intellectual pleasure, a purpose in life, work of some kind. But lacking any training or particular talent she felt frustrated, anxious and physically unwell. Her diary reveals her doubt and depression. 'March 1879: The old story of anaemia; want of employment, which makes life almost a torment, a silent misery. My life has been sadly wasted.' And two years later in April 1881 she wrote: 'Suffering acutely from absence of any occupation and from irritating restlessness.' Her sisters were worried about her, and in 1879 Theresa was writing to warn her against 'dreaminess which is apt to induce biliousness and low spirits and Heaven defend you from those old arch-enemies of the Heyworth–Potter nature'. Then there would be a change of mood and she would be drawn back into 'the whirlpool' of smart society. Even her determination not to 'come out' vanished after the pleasures of house parties and dances in Gloucestershire.

Superficially life was full of interest: there were so many

distractions and the family was never in one place for very long. In 1865 Richard Potter took a pleasant Jacobean house in Monmouthshire called The Argoed; it was easy to reach from Standish, and in addition to short visits – Laurencina considered it was her particular house – the family stayed there for a number of weeks each year. Fourteen years later Richard Potter also rented Rusland Hall, near Windermere in the Lake District, which was close to the timber-importing branch of his business at Barrow-in-Furness; and it was a convenient place for a late summer holiday after the Season was over in London. He travelled a great deal on business, and went regularly to North America. Since his wife declared herself too delicate to make the long and arduous journey he liked to take one or two of his daughters with him – a habit, thought Beatrice, that was partly due 'to a subconscious intention to keep out of less desirable associations'.

In September 1873 Beatrice was invited to go and she sailed from Liverpool with her sister Kate, her father and her brother-in-law Arthur Playne. While Richard Potter stayed in the Middle West to deal with the affairs of the Grand Trunk Railway the others went across to the Pacific coast, returning by way of Salt Lake City. All went wonderfully well for Beatrice, who wrote glowing accounts of the scenery, until she collapsed on the way back with scarlet fever, followed by rheumatic fever and then by measles. She lay ill in Chicago for six weeks. 'I wonder if I have altered,' she asked herself after the long and stressful expedition; 'and if altered whether for the better or the worse.'

In some ways her travels had only served to increase her dissatisfactions. 'My trip to America seems to have opened a new world to me,' she wrote in her diary. 'I am altogether unsettled and discontented ... getting into a nasty and indecent way of thinking of men, and love, and unless you take care,' she said to herself, 'you will lose all your purity of thought, and become a silly vain self-conscious little goose.' The physical impulses of adolescence greatly troubled

Beatrice and she turned to intellectual defences against her 'lower faculties' – and so began a persistent conflict between her reason and her feelings. The only cure, she decided, was to go heart and soul into religion; she conducted a correspondence with Theresa, the most religious-minded of the sisters, on the question of atonement. 'I wish my aim in life to be the understanding and acting up to Religion,' she wrote, and she was confirmed at Easter 1875. 'God grant that it may really strengthen me.'

Travel was one distraction. When Beatrice was twenty she went on a long visit to Germany and Austria with Mary and Arthur Playne, but they bored her; and she also hankered for the Season in London and worried about her health. In September 1879 she and her sister Maggie took off for a week's walking in the Lake District. 'Papa gave us £6 to do it upon,' Maggie recalled. 'Mamma saw no objection, but thought it slightly mean of me to take my £3 considering the size of my allowance. Much chaff about taking a hamper of provisions with us. Mamma hears of a certain leg of mutton that is likely to walk off; she declares it highly dishonourable after the £6 allowance, and conduct that only people with such lax religious opinions could possibly think of. Hereupon follows a fast and furious discussion upon the meaning of the word "religious". Beatrice indulges in one of her grand tirades of injured childhood, refers to Buddha and the ancient Egyptians and finally declares herself a most religious person. Mamma retreats to rally her forces for another onslaught and we retire to prepare for our expedition.'

Four years older than Beatrice, Maggie was the only one of the sisters with whom Beatrice enjoyed real intimacy and for a time they were like a married couple, said Beatrice, in their devotion to each other. Beatrice thought her the most intellectually gifted of all her sisters. 'Mamma is frightfully gloomy about our prospects generally,' Maggie wrote to Beatrice, 'so that one's only consolation lies in abstractions and books.' And so for a time they shared their interests, reading Ruskin and Goethe, discussing philosophy ancient and modern, enjoying long rides and walks together. Both of them were acquiring the reputation of being 'most strong-minded, blue-stocking young ladies', said Maggie, 'who could argue down the greatest arguer in the world'. Beatrice found her a most stimulating companion. 'I feel her loss terribly,' she wrote in 1879 when Maggie went off on an expedition with Herbert Spencer to Egypt, where they joined Kate. 'We are perfectly intimate and at one with each other and when I am with her I want no other society.' But a year later Maggie met Henry Hobhouse and they were married at Rusland in October 1880. Beatrice was alone once more.

An extended holiday in Italy seemed a congenial distraction and in the autumn of 1880 Beatrice set off for Turin, Perugia, Florence and Rome with a kindly solicitor and his wife, Mr and Mrs Cobb, for chaperones; she arranged to meet Theresa some weeks later and together to meet the Hobhouses in Rome on their honeymoon. 'I have been quite happy by myself, with the prospect of seeing the two girls in 3 or 4 days,' she wrote to her father when the Cobbs left for England. 'But I think my heart would have sunk within me if I had been staying the six weeks alone – and I should have had to resort to the confessional in St Peter's to relieve my feelings.' When Maggie wrote suggesting they meet in Florence rather than Rome Beatrice went to Cook's 'to engage a man to come to the station with me tomorrow and put me in charge of the guard'; she was considered to be a 'very enterprising young woman', and she herself, as she walked and drove about the city, felt rather surprised at her own independence. 'I have quite come to the conclusion that a sober-looking girl can do most things,' she told her father.

Theresa and Beatrice enjoyed the sights of Florence together and at Christmas they went on to Rome; 'we spent Xmas day in standing for 4 hours in bad air in St Peter's St Maria Maggiori – listening to rather indifferent music and

looking at very meagre processions.' Beatrice was nevertheless glad to be back in Rome: 'I expect to have a most delightful 11 weeks here,' she wrote. She was disappointed. She
found the climate varied disagreeably between depressing
heat and intense cold. She also found it painful to be with
Maggie again, who was now pregnant, and her presence
recalled their friendship now irretrievably gone. Her mother
was taken ill in January and Beatrice worried about her. And
then she herself was struck down with congestion of the lungs
and was consigned to be 'under a treatment of mixed poul-
tices and beef tea'. She wrote to her mother to say 'I think
I overdid myself in the last London Season and am gradually
working off the effects of it.' Theresa was a devoted nurse.
After a month confined to her room, when she read George
Eliot and Balzac, Beatrice decided she was well enough for
them to leave Rome and make their way to the Riviera. But
she was still out of sorts. 'I am afraid my lot in life is rather
to be a trouble than a pleasure to others,' she told her mother,
'but happily I am not responsible for my own existence, so
people must take me as I take myself, as a discipline in resignation and patience.' The holiday ended at Easter when she met
her parents in San Remo, but once the excitement of travel
and sightseeing was over Beatrice again relapsed into feelings
of dissatisfaction and self-disgust.

'I wish we could find a sufficiently charming husband for
Theresa,' Beatrice had written to her mother from Rome.
'She is looking so handsome and so young and sweet-looking.'
Nine months later Theresa, urged on by Beatrice, was
engaged to Alfred Cripps. As each of the sisters left home
Beatrice had to make a fresh adjustment, and at the prospect
of Theresa's marriage she wrote in her diary: 'The last of
sisterhood, at least of those of my generation, pledged herself!
... Now I am left alone, with this "problematical" younger
sister. ... These 24 years of my life now are nearly past and
gone – I know now pretty clearly what I ought to *do* (though
less than ever what I ought to think) and yet I cannot maintain

my reason as the ruler of my nature, but am still constantly enslaved by instinct and impulse.' She made an effort to keep in touch with her other sisters. 'One has to tighten the relations to one's married sisters when one is gradually being left alone in the home life,' she wrote to Mary Playne in September 1881.

There were also friends now to whom she was beginning to turn for comfort and companionship. At San Remo she had met Arabella Fisher, an intellectual woman who had made a 'sensible' late marriage to a retired colonial doctor. It was, however, her friendship with Mary and Charles Booth that she treasured most. Mary, born a Macaulay, was her cousin – 'a really remarkable woman, with an unusual power of expression, and a well-trained and cultivated mind'. For her part Mary Booth found Beatrice a strange girl. 'She is as odd as ever she can be,' she wrote to her husband after a visit from Beatrice in 1878. 'She is dreadfully bothered with the "weltschmertz", the uselessness of life etc. etc. I sympathised and comforted as well as I could. Then she went off, after the manner of the Potters, into a dissertation on the characters of her sisters.' Charles Booth was a ship-owner from Liverpool and when Beatrice first met him in the late Seventies she was intrigued by this tall, thin, delicate person who looked more like an ascetic priest than a man of business; he had in fact gone through a severe crisis of social conscience. Charles Booth had a mind of his own, rejecting orthodox views of politics and society. He was curious about the way people lived and how the social system actually functioned; he would often spend weeks away living in cheap lodgings in a poor quarter of Liverpool or London. When he settled in London after opening a branch of the family's ship-owning business in the City, he soon became aware of the growing ferment among the poor and the unemployed and the work of the philanthropic movement to alleviate misery.

As Beatrice came to know the Booths she not only found them 'exceedingly charming and lovable' but she enjoyed

their intellectual companionship. They were 'live wires' link-
ing her to the world of politics and philanthropy and she was
increasingly drawn to the idea of social service. But practical
work was not enough. She read a great deal of history, philosophy, esoteric religion and science. She studied mathematics
and geometry and filled her diary with long passages of
intellectual speculation. It was not an idle search for knowledge. She wanted to find a satisfactory religious faith for herself, a faith which was compatible with science. How could
service to God be fused with service to Man? She was beginning to think that she could best find fulfilment by taking
up the craft of social investigator.

Then in April 1882 all her hopes and plans fell to the
ground. Laurencina Potter died suddenly and Beatrice took
her mother's place as her father's hostess and counsellor, and
her younger sister's virtual guardian. Although Beatrice
grieved at the loss, she was for a time more at peace with
herself. Duty had given her a purpose in life and her new
responsibilities revived her energies. From being an anaemic
girl she became a healthy, vigorous woman. She was in a
state of exaltation all through the summer, which was spent
in Switzerland and Germany with her father, Rosie and Herbert Spencer. 'Goodbye the student! Enter the Society
Woman,' she wrote in her diary. All the same she was still
ambivalent. 'Shall I give myself up to society, and make it
my aim to succeed therein or shall I only do so as far as duty
calls me?' she was asking herself before the London Season
of 1883. 'On the whole the balance is in favour of society
... there is less presumption in the choice.'

But Beatrice soon became bored with the smart life. Talk
among society women about their servants and the daily
trivialities only irritated her. There were innumerable
decisions to be made about trifling matters – horses and
carriages to be transported and all the 'commissariat and para-
phernalia' for dinners, dances, picnics and week-end parties
to be provided. She hated herself for over-eating and

under-exercising. 'At present I feel like a caged animal,' she wrote in March 1883, 'bound up by luxury, comfort and respectability of my position. I can't get a training that I want without neglecting my duty.' She turned again to her studies for comfort and stimulation, and got into the habit of working between five and eight in the morning. 'Three hours of study are the happiest ones of the day,' she wrote. She arranged for lessons in physiology and for a time she did some work with her medical brother-in-law, Willie Cripps. These pursuits kept alive her ambition, and she was deterred only by a sense that her aspirations were greater than her intellect.

In April 1883 Beatrice joined the Soho Committee of the Charity Organisation Society which had been set up in 1869 to co-ordinate the innumerable agencies trying to help the poor; its aim was to induce a more self-respecting attitude among the recipients of charity. It was Kate who had introduced Beatrice into this world of philanthropy and it was while Beatrice was staying with her sister that she first became aware of the 'poverty of the poor'. Kate had been working as a rent collector at Katherine Buildings, a housing settlement inspired by Octavia Hill, one of the founders of the Charity Organisation Society. In March 1883 Kate married Leonard Courtney, the financial secretary to the Treasury in Gladstone's Government, and the ceremony was performed by her friend, Canon Samuel Barnett, at St Jude's Church in Whitechapel. Barnett, another of the founders of the COS, and his lively, pretty wife Henrietta were at the centre of the social reform movement. They set up Toynbee Hall for the education of working men, and ran it largely on the voluntary help given by young students and graduates from Oxford and Cambridge. Beatrice soon felt very much at home with these energetic, dedicated people: she found Barnett a man of 'fathomless sympathy', and his wife a woman of such gifts as to make her 'a veritable genius'. While she was fascinated by the work they were doing she was somewhat daunted by the problems. 'London is so huge and the poor are so helpless and ignorant,' she wrote after visits to the slums of Soho.

Divided between these new interests and the tasks of a London hostess, Beatrice began to feel that she was leading a double life – 'moving about men and women talking much as you are obliged to do and never mentioning those thoughts and problems which are your *real life* and which absorb in their pursuit and solution all the earnestness of your nature'. While it was understandable that such a beautiful and intelligent young woman of twenty-five should be one of the attractions of the Season, Beatrice had now learned to keep some of herself apart. 'I have had another ride with Sir John Lubbock,' she wrote to Mary Playne in July 1883 about this distinguished Liberal reformer whom she teasingly treated as an admirer, 'and he has sent me his last book, and asked me to tea with him any day I like to have on the terrace at Westminster. And so ends the London Season! and I shall return with clear social conscience to my dowdy dress (black lace and all), early hours and dear books.'

But Beatrice did not find it so easy as she had expected to take her mind away from London life in the autumn days at The Argoed. One of her new acquaintances that summer had been a neighbour at Princes Gate – Joseph Chamberlain.

CHAPTER TWO

Our Joe

IN 1883 Joseph Chamberlain was the rising star in the Liberal Party. This handsome, vigorous and strong-willed man, still under fifty, had caught the imagination of the country by bold radicalism. After he had made a considerable fortune in a family engineering business in Birmingham his ambitions and his public spirit quickly led him into politics. By 1873 he was Mayor of Birmingham, and three years later he became one of the city's Members of Parliament. In 1880 Gladstone put him in the Cabinet as President of the Board of Trade, and he began to make his national reputation with an impressive programme of social as well as political reform. He was a powerful and magically effective speaker. The citizens of Birmingham worshipped him as the man who put their city on the map. Everyone spoke of him as 'Our Joe'.

In private life, by contrast, Chamberlain was a reserved man. He had suffered a number of domestic misfortunes. In October 1863, when his wife died two years after their marriage on the birth of their second child, he was left to bring up little Beatrice and Austen. He married again in 1868 but, seven years later, his second wife also died in childbirth, leaving him with four more motherless children. He found it hard to recover from such blows of fate. 'This life is a damned bad business for me and I wish I were out of it,' he had told his colleague John Morley a year after the death of his second wife. His experience hardened him, and over the years he displaced his emotional energy into politics. Since the death of his wife, he told Charles Dilke in 1882, 'I have never worn my heart on my sleeve.' All the same, as success and popularity revived his spirits he began to go about again in society, and as one of the country's most eligible widowers he was on the look-out for a new wife.

When Beatrice met him at the beginning of June 1883 she was at first only casually interested in him. 'I do and I don't like him,' she wrote in her diary, deciding that talking to 'clever men in society is a snare and a delusion as regards interest. Much better read their books.' She met him again a few weeks later at a picnic given by a mutual friend at St George's Hill, Weybridge; she spent most of the afternoon talking to his daughter, Beatrice – 'a really genuine woman' – and her conversation with Chamberlain himself later that day provoked her curiosity, a feeling which was confirmed when she sat next to him at a dinner party on 18 July. 'Curious and interesting character,' she commented, 'dominated by *intellectual passions* with little self control but with any amount of *purpose*. How I should like to study that man!' Yet for all her growing interest she was determined not to become emotionally involved. 'My own individual life may be worthless,' she remarked, 'but today I feel as if I should regret it bitterly were I once to renounce it.'

At the end of September Beatrice was invited to spend a week with Chamberlain's daughter as a guest in the Chamberlain's London house. The young women were much of an age and they got on well together. Beatrice, moreover, learned much from her new friend about her father's character. 'Coming from such honest surroundings he surely *must* be straight in intention,' she concluded; even so she still was not quite sure that Chamberlain was trustworthy. 'Is the basis of those convictions honest experience and thought,' she asked herself, 'or were they originally the tools of ambition, now become inextricably woven into the love of power, and to his own mind no longer distinguished from it.'

For all her reservations Beatrice was beginning to think of him as a suitor. Mary Playne sent an encouraging letter. 'Your social and practical powers are considerable and you have ambition and self-control,' she wrote. 'I think you are well suited to a married life.' Since Mary had never approved of her sister's bookish ways she went on to warn her: 'What happiness did poor Mother's studies bring her? It is the melancholy tendency of such studies to separate people from their friends and neighbours.' Theresa took a different view about the possible match: 'If, as I hear from some quarters, Mr Joseph is on the look-out for a good wife and one who would forward, as you could do, his most ambitious views, don't you be carried away by any ambitious ideas yourself or any feeling that your life would be worth more in such a position than it is in the quiet pursuit of science which is *really* congenial to you,' she wrote. 'Look at the man himself as a man.'

To give herself a chance of knowing Chamberlain better Beatrice invited him to visit the family at The Argoed early in the New Year, though to inure herself against her feelings she looked for possible sources of difficulty. 'If as Miss C. says,' she told Mary in October, 'the Right Honourable Gentleman takes "a very conventional view of women" I may be saved all temptation by my unconventionality. I certainly shall not hide it. He would soon see that I was not the woman to "forward" his most ambitious views!'

Although the possibility of marriage would mean a change in her prospect of life as a single woman Beatrice still pressed on with her ambition to do useful work. She had already seen something of the down-and-outs of Soho and the East End, and the working of the Charity Organisation Society, but she had soon realized that she was no Lady Bountiful. She saw herself as a scholar, and she was determined to study as scientifically as possible the structure of society, particularly those sections of which she had no knowledge or experience. She wanted to see how the ordinary working people lived – 'mere philanthropists are apt to overlook the existence of an independent working class' – and with this in mind she decided to visit Bacup, the cotton-mill town in Lancashire where some of her mother's relations still lived, and to take the old family retainer, Martha Jackson – the beloved 'Dada' who belonged to that Bacup family – as a guide and companion. She would introduce herself simply as Miss Jones, a farmer's daughter from Monmouthshire, and in such a guise she would fit in better with these simple north-country people.

Beatrice had often heard her mother speak of her own childhood visits to these Bacup relatives – 'of her grandfather who would put on his old clothes to go to the Manchester market if times were good, and call on his wife to bring him his new hat and best coat if he felt his credit shaky; of the old grandmother sitting bolt upright in her wooden stays in her straight backed chair, giving sage advice to her four sons'. The grandparents were dead now but other relatives still lived and worked there. Beatrice soon felt completely at home among these warm-hearted people. She met a number of her grandmother's relatives, the Aked family; she visited the mills and the Co-operative Society which played such an important part in the life of the people and she talked to the mill-hands. 'Every evening I have my cigarette in a rocking chair by the kitchen fire,' she wrote, 'having persuaded my friends that all Welshwomen smoke.' They accepted her too – 'far more like a male than a female to talk wi'', one of them commented. 'Certainly the way to see industrial life is to live among the workers,' Beatrice wrote to her father. 'I am heartily glad I made the venture.'

The success of the Bacup visit strengthened her determination to make something of her own life, and she resolved not to be led astray. 'One thing I will *not* do,' she wrote in her diary on 7 December. 'I will not give way to a feeling, however strong, which is not sanctioned by my better self. I will not desert a life in which there are manifold opportunities for good for a life in which my nature is at war with itself.'

As Chamberlain's visit drew near she became increasingly anxious. 'My tortured state cannot long endure – the "to be or not to be" will soon be settled,' she wrote on 27 December. Years later when Beatrice looked back on this episode she realized that the excitement of the situation led her to precipitate a crisis long before there was any need for a decision – indeed she was so afraid that her feelings would overwhelm her better judgement that she provoked differences to divide them. At the time she was in a desperate state of conflict: 'this horrible dilemma which appears to threaten me (principle versus feeling) renders all my thought egotistical,' she wrote; 'perchance some current arising within the whirlpool will drift me outward. This truly is my last hope: if I do hope for continued independence of mind and body.'

Given such anxieties there was little chance of a successful courtship and the visit went badly from the start. There was an atmosphere of discomfort in the house, for no one quite understood why Beatrice had invited Chamberlain. It was clear, for instance, that Richard Potter did not care for his guest and he soon went back to a game of patience. He was 'utterly disgusted', Beatrice believed, 'at the *supposed* intentions of his visitor'. She described the visit in her diary in some detail.

At dinner, after some shyness, we plunged into essentials and he began to delicately hint his requirements. That evening and the next morning till lunch we were on 'susceptible terms'. A dispute over state education breaks the charm. 'It is a question of authority with women, if you believe in Herbert Spencer you won't believe in me.' This opens the battle. By a silent arrangement we find ourselves in the garden. 'It pains me to hear any of my views controverted,' and with this preface he begins with stern exactitude to lay down the articles of his political creed. I remain modestly silent; but noticing my silence he remarks that he requires 'intelligent sympathy' from women. 'Servility', Mr Chamberlain thinks I, not sympathy, but intelligent servility.... He tells me the history of his political career, how his creed grew up on a basis of experience and sympathy, how his desire to benefit 'the many' had become gradually a passion absorbing within itself his whole nature.... My aim in life is to make life pleasanter for this great majority. I do not care in the process if it become less pleasant for the well-to-do minority.

Beatrice was less impressed by the altruism of his ambitions than by the absence of any feelings towards her. 'He was simply determined to assert his convictions,' she wrote. 'I felt his curious scrutinizing eyes noting each movement as if he were anxious to ascertain whether I yielded to his absolute supremacy.' The next morning he suggested some more 'exercise'. 'I think both of us felt that all was over between us so that we talked *pleasantly* but even then he insisted on bringing me back from trivialities to a discussion as to the intellectual subordination of women.' Beatrice asked him bluntly: 'You don't allow division of opinion in your household, Mr Chamberlain?' 'I can't help people *thinking* differently from me,' he replied. 'But you don't allow the expression of the difference?' 'No,' he said. 'And that little word ended our intercourse.'

Beatrice was relieved when the visit was over, and she briskly turned her mind to other things. 'Plenty of practical work immediately in front of me,' she wrote. 'Undoubtedly the Bacup trip is the right direction. The time is come now for a defined object towards which all my energies must be bent.' The situation was not quite so clear-cut as she pretended to herself, for memories of Chamberlain's visit lingered and she had some second thoughts. 'Now that the pain and indecision are over,' she wrote, 'I can't help regretting that absorption in the peculiar nature of our relationship left me so little capable of taking the opportunities he gave me of knowing him.'

It was not long before a fresh opportunity arose to test her second thoughts. At the end of January she received an invitation to visit the Chamberlain family in Birmingham. 'Feeling convinced that the negotiation was off,' she explained to herself, 'I saw no harm in going to watch the great man at home.' Her first reaction was critical. She did not like Highbury, the ornate red-brick house which Chamberlain had built two years previously, and she found Beatrice Chamberlain and her aunt Clara sitting in the midst of ponderous luxury dressed with 'the dowdiness of the middle class'. There was a gloom, she thought, hanging over the home – 'no books, no work, no music, not even a harmless antimacassar to relieve the oppressive richness of the satin-covered furniture'.

She found it hard to maintain this aloof attitude, however, when she heard Chamberlain speak at a large political meeting that evening in the Town Hall, the high point of the visit. There were other Birmingham MPs on the platform including the well-loved Radical John Bright, but it was 'Our Joe' who was received with deafening shouts. As Beatrice listened to him speak and as she watched the devoted loyalty of his audience, in whom political convictions seemed to have taken the place of religious faith, she too was caught by the mesmeric quality of his passion, and she could not help but be impressed by the way he presented the interests of his people and his consideration of their weaknesses. She concluded that he undoubtedly had diplomatic talent, commenting wryly that 'the only case in which he does not show it is in *la recherche d'une femme*'.

The effect of the visit, despite her inclinations, was to draw Beatrice under Chamberlain's spell, and she used her diary to debate her contradictory feelings. 'I don't know how it will end. Certainly not in *my happiness*. As it is, his personality absorbs all my thought and he occupies a too prominent position for me not to be constantly reminded of him.' She still felt that the rational case against him was overwhelming. 'And if the fates should unite us (against my will) all joy and lightheartedness will go from me. I shall be absorbed into the life of a man whose aims are not my aims; who will refuse me all freedom of thought in my intercourse with him; to whose career I shall have to subordinate all my life, mental and physical.'

During the first months of 1884 Beatrice mulled over her feelings without coming any nearer to a solution. 'My own mind is not made up,' she confessed on 22 April. 'Practically I have resisted, have refused to take the line of subordination and absolute dependence which would have brought things to a crisis. Possibly my refusal to consent to the conditions will have cured all desire on the other side. Then though mortified I shall be relieved.' All the same she could not deny that 'his temperament and his character are intensely attractive to me. I feel I could relieve his gloom, could understand the mixed motives and the difficulties of a nature in which genuine enthusiasm and personal ambition are so curiously interwoven.' And, given the possible service to a great public figure, she felt bound to ask herself if she believed in the drift of his political views, and if the means employed were *honest*. Otherwise, she concluded, 'I should be selling my soul and should deserve misery.'

She conceded that Chamberlain 'has been straightforward all through, has told me distinctly his requirements'. And she recognized that the trouble lay within herself. She could not disguise her beliefs, but she felt wretched when she had to do so in order to please him. 'When I have been absolutely honest with him he has turned away. This is not what he wants and I *know* it,' she wrote; 'he has said in so many words "only devotion to my aims would justify you in accepting it". And I have not only no devotion to these aims but have to twist my reasoning in order to *tolerate* them.'

The straightest thing to do, Beatrice decided, would be 'to cut the knot by refusing all further intercourse'. And she turned to a sensible alternative: 'I shall look about me for some permanent work.' It was easier said than done, and even making up her mind to settle the matter upset her. 'I remain weak and discouraged,' she wrote at the beginning of May 1884. 'The woman's nature has been stirred to its depths: I have loved and lost.' Although she and Chamberlain met once or twice during the Season neither of them made any move to clarify their ambiguous situation. '*I* was not equal to it. But we have parted friends and understand each other.'

The frustration of the relationship left Beatrice feeling wretchedly unhappy and accentuated her loneliness. In the summer she went on holiday to Austria with Margaret Harkness, a relation who was in rebellion against an oppressive clerical family and was now living as a journalist on the fringe of London's literary and political bohemia. The distractions of sightseeing did not relieve Beatrice's distress: 'day and night I cried secretly over the past', she wrote in Munich. All she could do was to try to find a way of coping with her thwarted emotions. 'Today I say humbly we have learnt that we can neither see, think nor feel alone,' she declared; 'therefore we must live *for* others and take what happiness comes to us by the way. We must bear the self we have made.' Even so, she was still at a loss: 'if only I knew which way to turn'.

In November Beatrice had a visit from Chamberlain's sister Clara, who told Beatrice more of the family history including anecdotes of 'little Joe' in the nursery and schoolroom. 'It is a comfort to have come out of a painful affair with the respect and affection of his family,' Beatrice wrote to Mary afterwards, 'and to have done no harm anyway.' But this renewed association did nothing to dispel her depression and she recorded in her diary ominous feelings of approaching death. 'Personally it would be welcome. What would I give for a mother now; just to lay my head down, tell all – and cry. It is curious this feeling of life being ended.'

Work was a solace and a distraction as Beatrice put her energies into her new responsibilities in the East End. She had now taken Kate's place as a rent-collector at Katherine

Buildings, a long double-faced structure in five tiers, ribbed by open galleries. 'All the rooms were "decorated" in the same dull, dead red distemper,' said Beatrice, 'reminiscent of a butcher's shop.' Three narrow stone staircases led from the yard to the top-most gallery and on the landings were sinks and taps – three sinks and six taps to about sixty rooms. Behind a wooden screen were sets of six closets, sluiced every three hours; and these were used indiscriminately by the men, women and children, some six hundred in all, who inhabited the building. Such accommodation was no doubt an improvement on the slums it had replaced but this austere tenement was clearly a triumph of economy over benevolence. 'To treat one's neighbour as oneself,' Samuel Barnett caustically remarked, 'is not to decorate one's own house with the art of the world, and to leave one's neighbour's house with nothing but the drain-pipes to relieve the bareness of its walls.'

Beatrice took trouble to get to know the tenants, who quickly accepted her. She also came to like her fellow workers. One of them, a full-time social worker named Ella Pycroft, became a life-long friend. 'She and I are cut out to work with each other,' Beatrice told her father, 'as she has the practical ability and power to carry things through with steady work and I have more initiative and power of expression.' And as she came to know the Barnetts better she responded to their sympathy and encouragement. Henrietta Barnett was very anxious to raise the status of women, believing in both the equality and the differences of the sexes. 'And for that,' Beatrice told her, 'it will be needful for women with strong natures to remain celibate; so that the special force of womanhood – motherly feeling – may be forced into public work.' Now that Beatrice was a working woman – and Barnett was encouraging her to take on more responsibility – she developed a sympathetic understanding for the increasing number of women who had no prospect of a matrimonial career and sought a masculine reward for masculine qualities – what she called the 'unknown saints' who have a definite mission in life. 'I think these strong women have a great future before them – in the solution of social questions,' she told her father. 'I only hope that instead of trying to ape men and take up men's pursuits, they will carve out their own careers – and not be satisfied until they have found the careers in which their particular form of power will achieve most.'

Enthusiastic though she was about her new role in life Beatrice found it hard at times to maintain her determination. Her work, while stimulating and worthwhile, was sometimes dispiriting. 'When over-tired,' she wrote, 'the tenants haunt me with their wretched disorderly lives.' And for all her intentions, Beatrice could not break her connection with Chamberlain. For reasons she did not disclose the relationship again came to a crisis in early 1885. 'Tomorrow I shall know how my fate is to be unravelled,' she wrote on 29 January. 'No longer in my hands. If the answer be yes I am in honour tied. If no, I am free and *will be* free in body and mind – tomorrow will make thee a woman – a woman to love or a woman to work while others love.' But the next day, after she had seen Chamberlain, the moment of elation passed and she noted that 'this morning's talk seems like the dropping of the curtain over the tragic end of strong feeling'.

Her distress, and the cause of it, was becoming a matter of concern to Beatrice's relatives and her friends. She and Chamberlain met again in the Season of 1885; he dined with the Potters at York House, the mansion in fashionable Kensington Palace Gardens which had now become their London home. And then Kate Courtney, hoping to precipitate a decision, arranged a picnic in Buckinghamshire inviting Chamberlain specifically to meet Beatrice. 'That day will always remain engraved on my memory as the most painful one of my life,' Beatrice later recalled. 'The scene under the Burnham Beeches, forcing me to tell his fortune – afterwards behaving with marked rudeness and indifference. The great reception given to him at the station, returning back in the evening, we all running after him like so many little dogs.' She was ashamed of her own behaviour and disgusted with his; she decided she had no wish to see him again. Kate, too, was critical and she noted in her diary the 'detestable' tone of his political talk. 'I wonder what you thought of yesterday,' she wrote to Beatrice; 'to me there was no sign or trace of any other feeling than an intense personal ambition and desire to dominate at whatever cost to other people's rights. I do not even see any room in his nature for such an affection as would satisfy one of us. It would be a tragedy – a murder of your independent nature.' A few days later Kate's letter was followed by one from her husband, Leonard. 'I write partly because Kate's anxieties impel me,' he said, 'and partly because I shall greatly grieve at the fulfilment of a wasted endowment. Wit and the capacity of a noble life should not be sacrificed at meaner altars.'

Beatrice assured her family and friends that the matter was settled; 'my general impression coming home was a hopeless confusion – leading decidedly towards the negative', she wrote to Mary Playne after the picnic. 'The great man and I are painfully shy when we are alone and very anxious that nothing shall be noticed when others are there – a state of affairs which seems destined to lead to endless misunderstanding. It certainly brings a good deal of unhappiness to me – and I can't imagine *he* finds much amusement in it – I should think one or the other of us would break off this enigmatical relationship this autumn, by refusing to see more of each other.' Beatrice wrote to Mary Booth to the same effect. 'I can't tell you the feeling of relief your letter has given me,' Mary Booth replied, 'even in the midst of feeling sorry, very sorry,' she went on, 'for all this pain and disturbance. I do rejoice to know that the decision is "no". You never could be happy and would be increasingly unhappy with that man in such a relation to you.'

Up at Rusland for a Lakeland holiday Beatrice renewed

her determination to 'face a working life bravely and make the best of it', and she wrote to her sister Mary telling her that she had been thinking seriously about her future, 'especially about my relationship to Mr Chamberlain and I think I have arrived at definite conclusions. I certainly do not intend to be forlorn.' She forced herself back to an intellectual life, spending some of her holiday on a cultural stock-taking in aesthetics, philosophy and history. She was intrigued by the new socialist notions which were beginning to catch hold of young Radicals, and she planned a course of reading in social science. She was also working on a report to the trust which owned Katherine Buildings: 'I am working hard now at a book of all the tenants,' she told her father, 'past and present, with descriptions of occupation, family etc and statement of income, previous history, cause of leaving or ejectment.' With such a working programme there would be no time to mope. 'Tomorrow to London town to begin a new year of work,' she wrote when the holiday was over. 'I am back on the old lines,' she assured herself, but she also added the question: 'when shall I run off again?'

Beatrice went straight from the Lake District down to Whitechapel where, she told her father, she 'worked from 11 a.m. to 9 o'clock in the evening except for getting a hardly-cooked meal at a restaurant, slept there, and worked again from 9 to 1 o'clock and yesterday afternoon came back quite exhausted'. Her friendship with the Booths was both an emotional comfort and a support to her work, and during these difficult months they drew closer together. Charles Booth was turning his mind to a huge and detailed study of the London poor and he shared his thoughts with Beatrice when she stayed with them that summer. Mary, for all her domestic responsibilities, was equally excited by the plans for the survey, and she brought her discriminating mind to bear on the problems involved. She also provided a motherly support for Beatrice who had written anxiously when they were out of touch for a time that autumn. 'Give you up, or alter towards you! No. I will not,' wrote Mary Booth at once. 'Why should you fancy such things? Because you are not well, I fear, and out of spirits,' she went on. 'I wish I could come to see you. I am grieved that you suffer as you do: though the more I hear and read of that man the more satisfied I am of the rightness of your decision and the more thankful I am that you have made it.'

There were, nevertheless, continual reminders of Chamberlain that autumn, for the country was gripped by the fever of an election in which Chamberlain was energetically campaigning across the country for his new and controversial Radical programme. In October Beatrice had an invitation to visit from Chamberlain's sister, now Mrs Ryland: 'What has become of you, I wonder?' wrote Clara; 'I want you to come on November 2 and to stay until the Saturday.'

When Beatrice did visit her she was mortified to be told when she broke down in front of Clara Ryland that she was mistaken about the whole affair; and that the 'brother had never thought of me'. Beatrice was indignant at such duplicity. 'And this,' she wrote, 'after she had talked to me and examined me as to my intentions a year since.'

Beatrice was racked by teasing doubt and the strain was beginning to tell on her. In search of relief she went to spend three days with Mary Booth but she was upset by the continual conversation. 'I am constantly weary,' she wrote on 8 November; 'life is a continual struggle – a real battlefield, both physically and mentally. Still,' she added hopefully, 'this gnawing pain will cease – in time. I have not yet fully realised the *uselessness* of it.'

CHAPTER THREE

A Working Woman

'It is curious what an ominous feeling I have had lately – as if something terrible were about to happen,' Beatrice wrote to her father early in 1885. On 26 November her fears were realized. It was polling day in London and when Richard Potter went out to vote that morning he was struck down with a paralytic stroke. Although he partially recovered, remaining cheerful and mentally lucid, for the rest of his life he claimed more of Beatrice's time and energies. She despaired as she thought over the prospect of caring for this old invalid as well as her depressed and ailing sister Rosie. 'The future does look gloomy indeed. Good God, how awful! This time last year I was suffering from the same feeling – with other circumstances. There was hope for me then in work. Now I am *hopeless.*'

All her plans were shattered by this blow. For a start she would have to abandon her work in the East End and since the doctors advised that Richard Potter should be taken out of London, the old smart style of life at home was also finished. Until suitable arrangements could be made Beatrice took her father to stay with Mary and Arthur Playne at their country house, Longfords, not far from the old family home in Gloucestershire. As Beatrice brooded over her plight through Christmas and the New Year she sank into desperate depression. On New Year's Day 1886, 'in case I should not outlive the year', she made her will. 'If Death comes it will be welcome – for life has always been distasteful to me.' As the weeks passed she could not shake off her sense of desolation. 'I am never at peace with myself now – the whole of my past looks like an irretrievable blunder – the last two years like a nightmare,' she wrote in her diary on 11 February. 'I struggle through each new day – waking with suicidal thoughts trying to beat back Feeling into the narrow rut of duty. Religion, Love and Ambition have died.' She felt imprisoned by her suffering. 'When will pain cease?' she asked in her misery.

Early in February, as soon as her father was well enough to be moved, Beatrice took him to convalesce in the mild climate of Bournemouth. It was much less of a strain to care for him in this seaside resort than it was in London, she reported to Mary, for there was 'nothing and nobody to distract my attention and no chain of excitement for him'; and in any case it was a good time to get away from the smoke and the fog and the tumult of London. Times were very bad, in the coldest winter for thirty years, and the docks and building trades had come to a stop. There was hunger and anger in the alleys of the East End, and there were rumours of revolution. On 8 February over twenty thousand men, mostly unemployed dockers and building labourers, attended a mass meeting in Trafalgar Square, and at its end a section of the crowd surged into Pall Mall and marched past the smart clubs which lined that street. The clubmen stood at the windows and jeered at the demonstrators; the mob retaliated by throwing stones, breaking windows, pillaging the jewellers and looting the wine shops. The socialist leaders, John Burns and Henry Hyndman, were no more able to control this orgy of violence than the police, and for the next two hours the crowd rampaged through the West End, overturning carriages in Hyde Park and drunkenly singing 'Rule Britannia' as they drifted back along Oxford Street to the slums of East London.

That riot was a nightmare for the middle classes, and it was followed by two days of fear. Shops, offices and even private houses were barricaded, and the troops put on the alert, as rumours of marching columns spread through a dense fog which blanketed London. Nothing came of this spontaneous outburst, and London returned to normal. But the shock had focused attention on the plight of the poor, and thousands of pounds were given to a relief fund set up by the Lord Mayor. There was also much talk of relief work for the unemployed. Some social workers were opposed to indiscriminate help, believing that it would demoralize the better class of worker and encourage the improvidence of the feckless, and there was much argument on this point. Beatrice sent a letter to the *Pall Mall Gazette*, a liberal newspaper edited by the clever W. T. Stead, who was a pioneer of sensational journalism, and he proposed to publish it as an article. It appeared on 18 February under the title of 'A Lady's View of the Unemployed', and Beatrice was delighted by this little success which gave her the encouragement she needed to go on with her studies and her writing. It was, she wrote across Stead's letter of acceptance, 'a turning point in my life'.

The letter attracted some notice, and among those who read it was Chamberlain. He wrote to Beatrice, and as soon as she saw his handwriting she felt 'ominously excited'. Any reminder of her feelings was disturbing. 'I knew it was the old torture coming back again,' she noted. Chamberlain was personally intrigued by her opinions, and he was also politically concerned, for as President of the Local Government Board he was the member of the Cabinet largely responsible for dealing with the severe trade depression and the sudden increase in the number of workless men. He therefore asked Beatrice to come and see him. 'I read your letter with great interest and agreement and should very much like to know more of your experiences.' Beatrice replied with a formal businesslike letter from Bournemouth. 'I am very sorry that I am out of London and unable to benefit by your kindness in wishing to see me,' she wrote; and she went on to expand her views, modestly declaring that her knowledge was only superficial but nonetheless making a useful suggestion that foreshadowed the labour exchanges of the future. Chamberlain replied at once. 'I know that you have much experience,' he insisted, 'and you will find me ready to profit by your suggestions.' He was prepared for more state intervention than she was. 'I cannot think that any registration of labour would be more than a trifling convenience,' he wrote in reply to her suggestion. 'Whenever there is work wanted, workers will find it out very quickly for themselves. If the distress becomes greater something *must* be done to make work. The rich must pay to keep the poor alive.'

Beatrice, always quick to sense a slight, sent him a frigid reply. 'As I read your letter, a suspicion flashed across me that you wished for some further proof of the incapacity of a woman's intellect to deal with such larger matters.' She also disagreed with him politically for she was still under the influence of Herbert Spencer's stern individualism, which taught that every man must do his best without help from the State. 'I have no proposals to make,' she told Chamberlain in this spirit, 'except sternness from the State, and love and self-devotion from individuals.' And then she came back to her nagging doubts about his motive in writing to her. 'But is it not rather unkind of you to ask me to tell you what I think? I have tried to be perfectly truthful. Still, it is a ludicrous idea that an ordinary woman should be called upon to review the suggestions of Her Majesty's ablest minister, especially when I know that he had a slight opinion of even a superior woman's intelligence in these matters (I agree with him) and a dislike of any independence of thought.'

Beatrice seemed bent on making reasonable relations between them impossible by such mock-modesty and sarcastic references back to her earlier arguments with Chamberlain about the position of women and his insistence on male supremacy in his household. 'I thought that he wished to know my mind literally to see whether it would suit him,' she wrote defensively in her diary when she entered the stiff-backed reply which this admittedly 'pedantic' letter evoked from Chamberlain. 'I thought we understood each other pretty well,' he wrote next day, 5 March. 'I fear I was mistaken. You are quite wrong in supposing that I undervalue the opinion of an intelligent woman. There are many questions on which I would follow it blindly.' He also rebutted her other charge. 'Neither do I dislike independence of thought.' Yet he was clearly stung to the point where any further exchanges were pointless. 'I hardly know why I defend myself,' he wrote, 'for I admit that it does not much matter what I think or feel on these subjects.' He came to a curt ending: 'I thank you for writing so fully and do not expect any further answer.'

Though Beatrice had brought this snub upon herself she felt so pained and bitter that she broke through the conventional niceties of such a correspondence. 'Now I see I was right not to deceive you,' she wrote to Chamberlain in the agony of the moment. 'I could not lie to the man I loved. But why have worded it so cruelly, why give unnecessary pain? Surely we suffer sufficiently. Thank God! that when our own happiness is destroyed, there are others to live for. Do not think that I do not consider your decision as *final* and destroy this.'

'Is it ended now?' Beatrice wondered in her diary, where she had placed a copy of the letter she sent to Chamberlain. 'I think so.' She tried to analyse what lay at the heart of the trouble. 'Double-mindedness has run right through,' she concluded: 'a perpetual struggle between conscience on the one hand and feeling on the other – not had the courage to follow either to the bitter end – hence my misery. And on his side hatred of insubordination and personal attraction possibly tinged with pity for I believe the man believed I loved him – so I did! And now these last words from me close it. God help me.'

In the spring days at Bournemouth she grew calmer and she felt comforted in doing her family duty and thinking of her public work, still determined, if she could, to devote her life to social problems. In the aftermath of her exchange with Chamberlain, and touched by memories of her youthful religious struggles when she was a schoolgirl at Stirling House in Bournemouth, she again turned to religion for comfort as she had after the death of her mother; 'for the first time I live harmoniously with myself', she noted, as gradually the bleak suicidal despair left her. 'It will be a sad life,' she decided. 'God grant it may be a useful one – that I may dedicate myself earnestly and without trembling to a search after the truths which will help people. My way of life has been chosen for me; let me walk on it with an open mind and a single heart. God grant it.'

In this chastened mood Beatrice returned to London. It was April 1886 and a time of crisis in Chamberlain's political fortunes. Since the election in the autumn he had increasingly been at odds with Gladstone and most of his Cabinet colleagues. He was not only arguing for a more radical programme of social reform than most of the Liberal leaders were prepared to accept but he had fallen out with Gladstone over the Prime Minister's plan for Home Rule in Ireland – a measure which Chamberlain thought so dangerous and disruptive of Imperial unity that he was prepared to resign and split the Liberal Party rather than accept it. His resignation in March led to a series of heated debates in the House of Commons and on one of these great occasions Beatrice was in the gallery to hear Chamberlain, 'pale and nervously excited', plead his case. In the past Beatrice had been contemptuous of his egotism and self-satisfaction. Now that he was sacrificing his future for his principles she saw him in a more sympathetic light; and her fascination with him was as strong as ever. Mary Booth, who had never cared for Chamberlain, again tried to console Beatrice. 'A man so dependent on flattery, so impatient of contradiction, so sensitive

39

with regard to his own feelings, and so indifferent to those of others must be at bottom a very poor and shallow creature,' she wrote. 'You are well rid of him.' 'I fear I shall never think of him as you do,' Beatrice replied sadly.

Mary Booth was much more encouraging about Beatrice's intellectual talents and she welcomed the help Beatrice proposed to give her husband in his ambitious social survey. In April, moreover, Charles Booth invited Beatrice to join a Board of Statistical Research. He wanted to discover how much real poverty there was among the four million inhabitants of London. How did the poor really live? What did they really want? Booth wished to relieve the sense of helplessness that he and other well-intentioned people felt in the face of widespread and dangerous misery. 'We need to begin with a true picture of the modern industrial organism,' he declared; 'the problems of human life must be better stated.'

The idea was to begin work in the East End of London, which had one million ill-fed, ill-educated inhabitants, many of whom were living in huddled and disease-ridden tenements and struggling to survive on low wages and casual work. No one knew the exact extent of this poverty and Booth proposed to survey a cross-section of this population to map the social ills of the poor. Beatrice was fascinated by the idea: 'It is just the sort of work I should like to undertake, if I were free,' she wrote in her diary. She had always been drawn to broad-based beneficence rather than individual charity. And Herbert Spencer had taught her that it might be possible to apply scientific methods to the study of society. This sociological bias, touched by an awakening conscience, made her wish to find the root cause of a general problem in the hope of finding a general answer. 'To me "a million sick" have always seemed actually more worthy of self-sacrificing devotion than the "child sick of a fever" preferred by Mrs Browning's Aurora Leigh,' she wrote. While Beatrice could not leave her father long enough to do much practical work for the survey she felt she could improve her capabilities by studying economics and coming to grips with the ideas of leading economists with a view to writing an article on the subject; and during the spring weeks, temporarily relieved from her domestic ties, she went off to work at the British Museum.

Despite the worries and responsibilities of family life Beatrice struggled to assert her independence, and she still alternated between visits to the East End, the British Museum and the usual dinners and receptions of the London Season. She enjoyed such weeks of freedom. As she went about alone in society she began to see the threat that women like herself might be to the traditional scheme of things. 'Let men beware of the smoking woman,' she mused. 'I would urge earnestly on the defenders of Man's supremacy to fight the female use of tobacco with more sternness and vigour than they have deployed in the female use of the vote. It is a far more fatal power. It is the wand with which the possible women of the future will open the hidden stores of knowledge of men and things and learn to govern them. Then will women become the leading doctors, barristers and scientists. And a female Gladstone may lurk in the dim vistas of the future.'

Beatrice returned from London to find that Rosie was again in a weak, hysterical state and she took her two invalids off to The Argoed where she planned to read and study. Now that she had decided to live her own intellectual life, and despite the demands of her sick sister and father was finding ways of doing so, her spirits rose. 'I am happy, happier than I have been for three long years, mostly spent in egotistical misery,' she was able to write at the end of June. 'I am thoroughly enjoying my life,' she went on: 'I am living in the present and preparing for the future.' She worked hard through the summer, reading Adam Smith, J.S. Mill, Ricardo and Walter Bagehot, Stanley Jevons and Alfred Marshall. She admitted that 'political economy is *hateful* – most hateful drudgery', but she was determined to master it. 'I must love my work and not myself,' she declared, 'follow truth on my knees, humbly.' There were only moments of regret: 'Ah! but Love, how much sweeter than Truth.'

And so the summer days passed away pleasantly with work, visits from friends and country walks with Don, her St Bernard dog. In August she invited Beatrice Chamberlain to stay with her. The two young women had seen something of each other in London and Beatrice could not help finding it 'a painful happiness to be with her'. Miss Chamberlain told her how much the strains of the past few months had aged her father and Beatrice was touched by the way in which the girl idealized him. 'I could not have idealised that man,' she said to herself, 'though I loved him so passionately. Only to a *Faith* could I bring the whole devotion of my nature. Still, for all that, God bless him!'

By the end of the summer she had finished her article which she called 'The Rise and Growth of English Economics'. She was proud of her achievement but she could not help wondering whether 'if it is published it will be thought very conceited? It isn't so. It is this hopeless independence of thought that makes my mind so distasteful to many people and rightly so, for a woman should be more or less dependent and receptive. However I must perforce go through the world with my mind as it is and be *true to myself.'* In this more cheerful, confident mood she planned her work. 'The winter is to be devoted to German socialism,' she decided, 'and then for English history but this time with a definite intention of writing a history of Industrialism or something of the sort. Ah work, what a great comfort it is.'

As Beatrice adjusted to her new way of life she was aware of the changes within herself and the effect of her new ambitions upon her personality. She now saw herself as 'a working woman who has lived through passion and pain – and come out of it with only a kind of hopeless faith, and stern determination to do her little best and die'.

She was energetically sociable. In October she dashed off to Birmingham to stay with Clara Ryland who was looking after Highbury while her brother was away. 'I was glad to see the house again – the home of my hero. Now I can think of the whole story calmly and see how I was led away by the excitement around me – long before there was any need for decision. It is better as it is. I wish him nothing but good.' Yet for all her seeming detachment she was still asking 'will the pain of it ever cease?' She went down to Brighton to see Herbert Spencer who was busy writing his autobiography, and she learned that the old savant had named her his literary executor. In London she had lively evenings with the Booths talking with them till midnight. Then at the end of October she paid another visit to Bacup and she was again impressed by this simple community, focused round the chapel and the Co-operative store. 'I am more and more charmed with the life of these people,' she wrote to her father, 'with their warm-hearted integrity and power to act together.' They were teaching her as much about the social fabric as she learned from Booth and her academic studies of political economy.

Back in London her mood changed; once more she was afflicted by her old melancholy, brought on by all the painful associations of York House: 'the lot I have drawn in life,' she complained, 'is an evil-omened number'. She went on to Bournemouth at the beginning of December but found nothing there to cheer her. Her father seemed to be weaker, Rosie was a 'sodden weight', Miss Darling, the household companion, was depressing and small-minded, and Beatrice, after ten days of hard work with Karl Marx, ended with a cold in bed. 'Why this ceaseless grasping after that phantom – happiness,' she asked herself. 'And, as the only alternative, why this desperate clutch at Power – power to impress and to lead. No wonder I gain only a powerless unhappiness.'

As she brooded about herself she decided that, like her mother, she had a duplex personality; there was a 'nether being in me: the despondent, vain, grasping person (the Heyworth) doomed to failure, gloomily religious whose natural

43

vocation and destiny was the convent'. The other personality was 'light-hearted' and 'an enthusiast for Truth' with its 'life and origins in my sensual nature'. If only she were a man, she felt, her 'strong physical nature would be satisfied', but 'as I am a woman these feelings unless fulfilled in marriage, which would mean destruction of the intellectual being, must remain controlled and unsatisfied finding their only vent in the nethermost personality, religious exhaltation'. She had experienced her mother as a frigid woman and there was no way in which she could associate love and passion with the feminine side of her nature. She felt herself to be in an irreconcilable dilemma, unable to satisfy both her intellectual and her sensual needs. At last she decided that 'womanly dignity and reserve side with Fate and forbid the inroads of Passion'. And so the old year wore itself out sadly. All Beatrice could say was that she was somewhat happier than she had been a year before.

As the critical phase of Richard Potter's illness passed and he settled into a routine, Beatrice felt it was no longer necessary for her to be so closely on hand and her married sisters insisted that they should take their share of looking after him. Although Beatrice had a strong affection for her sisters – they were in constant touch with visits and dinners and letters – she sensed an increasing intellectual gulf; they were all so different from her in their aims in life and had little sympathy either with her ideas or her ambitions. 'Why don't you live like other people,' Georgina asked with characteristic bluntness, 'instead of pretending to be a genius?' The sisters had always thought that Beatrice was rather priggish. 'What nonsense is this,' Mary had told her years before, 'trying to be a blue-stocking when you are meant to be a pretty woman.'

All the same the older sisters wanted her to lead her own life, and it was agreed that she should be free for at least four months in the year to travel or work or amuse herself. Beatrice had no doubt what she would do. Charles Booth was now absorbed in his inquiry, working in the evenings with three paid secretaries. Beatrice offered to make her own contribution with a study of life among the dock workers of the East End and she started on the task during her Easter holiday in 1887. Her work brought her closer to the Booths and she often visited them in London or at Gracedieu, a large grey house on the edge of Charnwood Forest in the Midlands which the family had taken in 1886. Both the Booths thought highly of Beatrice's capacities – they had responded with encouragement and admiration to her article on economics even though, to her disappointment, they advised against its publication until she had clarified her ideas further. 'Beatrice has the power,' Mary Booth wrote to her husband, 'of investigating what she takes up with charm. She has a genuine enthusiasm and can impart it.' Charles Booth found her an intelligent colleague in the work of the survey and they spent long hours in discussion together. Beatrice in turn grew more affectionate and fond. 'They become each year more near to me,' she wrote. 'Perhaps they are the only persons who really *love* me.'

Beatrice, like her sisters, had always been a forthright person, unafraid of expressing her opinions and falling easily into argument. As she studied, her opinions changed – the individualism of Herbert Spencer gave way to a belief in a more controlled society. She was moving from an earlier conservatism towards a paternalistic socialism without even passing through a period of Liberalism; and as she grew more confident she became more dogmatic, given to an aggressive gaucherie in her determination to make herself felt. Margaret Harkness told her that she was 'unattractively combative'. And although Beatrice was honest enough to agree with this criticism she observed 'how difficult it is to be both earnest and eager as well as adaptable and womanly!' In February 1887 she travelled down to Cornwall with the Courtneys and Sir George Trevelyan who had been invited down to speak for Leonard Courtney in his constituency at Liskeard. Beatrice entered eagerly into the political conversations and she soon realized that the originality of her views often led to talk at cross-purposes. She talked with a sympathetic local farmer, a deeply religious man who, she felt, was sentimental about the poor – 'our conversation another instance of the entire novelty of the scientific view of society – of the hopeless misunderstanding of the motto (my motto) to *know in order to act*. According to these excellent persons it is individual suffering that must be relieved not the common good considered. And I maintain that I am the *true socialist*, through my willingness to sacrifice the individual to the community.' And coming home in the train with Trevelyan she felt the gulf between this cultured and cultivated gentleman and her own life. 'No wonder he failed to understand me when I tried to explain to him the pathos and sometimes the beauty of the life and character of the failure – the charm of the cosmopolitan intercourse of the London life of the professional and working classes.'

Beatrice's suffering had, in fact, not only affected her personality; it had also played a part in changing her social and political attitudes. She was now gradually losing her taste for the smart world of London, and her ventures into social life that Season only confirmed her feeling that 'it is not worth while to know Society – to meet it occasionally makes me feel how little I lose in being out of it'. Instead she spent much of the spring working on her inquiry into dock life. With her friend and colleague Ella Pycroft she entertained social workers and other professional people employed in the East End and she mused on what 'the conventional West End acquaintances would say to two young women smoking and talking in the bed-sitting, working, smoking, bathroom of an East End school board visitor'.

Beatrice was increasingly absorbed in her work and in the new friendships associated with it, yet she was still unable to shake off the spell which Chamberlain had cast upon her. Since their correspondence in February 1886 he had made several attempts to renew their acquaintance either directly

or through his family. Then on 19 May 1887 he sent her a
letter. 'By a curious co-incidence I met Mr Booth at breakfast
at your sister's yesterday morning. I had not then read his
paper or I should have liked to have some talk with him about
it. It gives a most interesting picture of life at the East End
and on the whole a more hopeful one than I had supposed
possible. What is to be done for these people? Organised and
wise charitable interventions – which will not do more harm
than good – seem impossible on a large scale. What can
Government do? State employment would give rise to every
form of jobbing and extravagance and would interfere with
business and private enterprise. I do not see my way at all
and yet I fear that the problem may at any moment be forced
upon us in an acute form.'

And so began 'another act of the old old story'. At the beginning of June Beatrice was again in Birmingham to hear
the great man speak. It was a difficult period in Chamberlain's
career; he had decisively split his party over Home Rule for
Ireland and he was now struggling to retain his hold upon
his local supporters in order to keep his place in public life.
Beatrice noted how different was the atmosphere from the
'intoxicating enthusiasm' of four years before; the crowd was
smaller and the tone of his speech was less arrogant. 'Sentimental sympathy for the wrongs of the down-trodden
masses was exchanged for a determination to preserve law
and order. The statesman had overcome the demagogue.'
Beatrice, sitting only a few steps away from him, thought
that for all his pale, agitated appearance he had lost none of
his old charm of voice and manner. After he sat down, she
noted 'it was natural our eyes should meet in the old way'.
For all the change of sympathy, however, they were still unable to come to a better understanding. Beatrice refused an
invitation to a political dinner at Highbury, but she did meet
Chamberlain at the house of his brother, Arthur Chamberlain. Once again she was ambivalent. She felt that he did not
treat her with respect – 'he behaved towards me as the

triumphant lover'; and yet she was 'weak and romantic' enough to invite him to The Argoed later in the summer. There the tantalizingly provocative relationship continued. On this occasion Beatrice's emotions got the better of her 'womanly dignity'; at last her pride gave way to her feelings and she told Chamberlain how deeply she cared for him but at the same time insisting that they should not see each other again. Put in this difficult position, Chamberlain preserved his emotional distance, saying again that he wished her to be his friend. For Beatrice, however, it had to be one thing or the other. Unable to bear her racking conflict she sent a letter intended to break off the relationship for good. Chamberlain replied on 7 August.

Dear Miss Potter,

I thank you sincerely for your kind letter. I can not help feeling depressed and discouraged at times and I value greatly the sympathy which you have shown me.

The concluding part of your letter has given me much pain. Did I indeed do wrong in accepting your invitation? If so forgive me and allow me to tell you frankly what I feel. At your own request I destroyed your letter of March 1886. There was one passage in it on which I did not presume to put a definite interpretation, and which I thought at the time was rather the outcome of a sensitive mind, overstrained by suffering and work, than the expression of settled feeling. I thought you had forgotten it and wished me to forget it also.

So much for the past – now as to the future. Why are we never to see each other again? Why can we not be friends – 'camarades' – to use your own expression? I like you very much – I respect and esteem you – I enjoy your conversation and society and I have often wished that fate had thrown us more together.

If you share this feeling to any extent why should we surrender a friendship which ought to be good for both of us?...

The circumstances of my past life have made me solitary and reserved, but it is hard that I should lose one of the few friends whose just opinions I value and the sense of whose regard and sympathy would be a strength and support to me.

I cannot say more. You must decide, and if it is for your happiness that we should henceforth be strangers I will make no complaint.

I return your letter, as you wish it, but there is surely no reason why you should be ashamed of feelings which are purely womanly and for which I have nothing but gratitude and respect.

I am always yours very sincerely,

J. Chamberlain.

Chamberlain's letter did nothing to break the barrier between them; it only made Beatrice angry. 'This letter,' she wrote in her diary, 'after I had, in another moment of suicidal misery, told him I cared for him passionately. This after he had pursued me for 18 months and dragged me back into an acquaintance I had all along avoided. To insist on meeting a woman who had told you she loved you in order to humiliate her further.' This visit had only produced more unhappiness to add to the long chain of misery, and Beatrice turned to the Barnetts, the Booths and the Courtneys to restore her spirits. 'I must endeavour to get in front of my own shadow,' she declared, 'else I shall end by disbelieving in sunshine.'

And so ended this strange relationship, full of held-back feelings and scarcely articulated intentions. Chamberlain was plainly attracted to Beatrice as an intelligent and handsome wife for a widower much in the public eye, but he was never enamoured of her; a younger, more passionate man might have overcome her inhibitions, and an older man who was infatuated might have swept her off her feet. A proud and wilful personality, he was clearly unwilling to compromise when he clashed with similar facets of Beatrice's imperious nature. Their spasmodic attempts to find a common ground thus became a trial of strength rather than a courtship, for neither could or would give way.

As a working woman Beatrice was making progress. At the end of September her research into 'Dock Life in the East End' was published as an article in the *Nineteenth Century*. She was pleased about that. Although she felt that she had no 'talent' and was almost lacking 'literary faculty' she recognized that she had 'originality of aim and method – and I have a sort of persistency which comes from despair of my own happiness'. York House was given up that autumn – it was no longer needed as Richard Potter now spent most of the winter at Bournemouth and Rosie was 'on a fair way to matrimony'. Beatrice was learning to be philosophical about life. 'Tho I have made an awful mess of it,' she told Mary Playne, 'I shall find a sort of resigned satisfaction to work and intend to be a comfortable sort of failure. It is no use crying over spilt milk, whether it be matrimony or eternal spinsterhood.'

CHAPTER FOUR

A Mission in Life

'I HAVE lived through my youth – it is over,' Beatrice wrote at the beginning of November 1887 when she was back in the comfortable lodgings at Bournemouth. 'But I am only on the threshold of working womanhood.'

She was now nearly thirty and had at last found a life that suited her, one in which 'I can be most use to my fellow mortals'. Before she left London to spend the winter with her father she had agreed to go on working for Charles Booth; her next project was to be a study of the Sweating system, whereby a middleman put out piece-work, usually to women, in their own tenements or in squalid 'sweatshops' in the East End. As the name implied, long hours and wretched pay had given this system an evil reputation, and Beatrice believed that she could only get at the facts by first-hand experience. She decided to concentrate on a study of Sweating in the tailoring trade, which played such an important part in East End life, and to do this effectively she would have to disguise herself and go among the workers as she had done during her visit to Bacup four years earlier.

To prepare herself for this adventure she first tried to learn some of the skills and jargon of the trade: the most she could do, with her accent, manners and experience, was to pass herself off as a genteel woman who had fallen on hard times. The work was customarily divided into specialities.

There were women who did nothing but buttonholes, or basting, or finishing. Beatrice chose to learn the work of a trouser-hand. 'I worked four days with the Moses family, and we parted excellent friends,' she wrote. 'The work must have been bad, for my sewing, they said, was too good for the trade.'

While Beatrice was staying at the Devonshire House Hotel in Bishopsgate, a temperance establishment that she made her London base after her father gave up York House, she took the chance to learn all she could about Sweating by getting her colleagues on the Booth enquiry to provide reports on tailoring workshops along the Mile End Road, by interviewing factory and sanitary inspectors, and going out to talk to small employers and workers. And after she returned to Bournemouth she spent the autumn and winter months on more research. 'All the volumes, blue books, pamphlets and periodicals bearing on the subject of Sweating that I could buy or borrow were read and extracted,' she wrote. This steady work for a purpose was a source of relief to her stressed emotions. 'The first Xmas for five years that I have been in a peaceful happy frame of mind,' she wrote on Christmas Day 1887.

In the early spring when her regular leave from her domestic cares came round, Beatrice went back to pursue her inquiries in the East End. Dressing herself for the part, she got herself taken on as 'a plain trouser-hand'. The work was unrewarding in every sense. 'Work as hard as one may,' Beatrice concluded, 'one cannot make much over 1/- a day.' She was clearly inexperienced and different in style from her workmates, who were given to a stream of coarse badinage about sexual promiscuity and perversion. Yet she found the other women friendly, willing to help her although time cost them money and ready to share with her their hard-earned refreshments. Beatrice even came to feel sorry for the much-criticized middleman, seeing that he was just as much a victim of the system as the women he employed. As far as the work

was concerned it was soon clear that Beatrice was out of her
depth, but she evoked respect and one kindly employer told
her that 'a tidy-looking person like you' ought to get some
respectable man to marry her; 'you're more fit for that than
to be making your own living in this sort of place'. In any
case, after a few days' work she had all the material she needed
for an article for the *Nineteenth Century*, so she abandoned
her disguise and went back to more conventional forms of
social investigation.

In April 1888 Beatrice went to the House of Commons
to hear Chamberlain speak, now as a supporter of the Conservative Government which his defection from the Liberal
Party had helped to bring to power, and she found that
the sight of him no longer upset her. 'My present life,' she
decided, 'though lonely and at times wearisome, is better
than it would have been by his side.' Even when the newspapers carried rumours that Chamberlain was engaged to
Mary Endicott, a young American who was the daughter
of the U.S. Secretary of War, she was able to keep control
of her feelings. 'A gasp – as if one had been stabbed – and
then it is over.'

In the summer months of 1888, which Beatrice spent with
her father at The Argoed, she was still adjusting herself to
the idea of life as a working spinster. 'And now I am left alone
– the last and only Potter,' she noted when Rosie was married
from the house at the end of August. As Beatrice gave herself
up to her 'special mission – of duty to society at large rather
than to individuals', her mind often turned back to memories
of her mother, feeling closer to her and more loving than
she had ever done, and once again she felt the fusion of dedication to useful work and of religious sentiment which
amounted to a vocation. When she was in London she would
walk round to St Paul's and draw comfort from its quiet
space; and she found an equally soothing benefit in the peace
of the steep-sided valley of the Wye that ran below the
garden of The Argoed. 'I have been wounded,' she wrote,

'horribly wounded – and the scar can never leave me.' It seemed to her like a period of initiation into a new life.

In August the *Nineteenth Century* published the first of her articles on Sweating called 'Pages from a Work Girl's Diary' which was a minor sensation and its good reception buoyed her spirits. She was gradually gaining a professional reputation – in May she gave evidence before the House of Lords Committee on Sweating. She was asked to speak at a women's trade-union meeting, and she wrote long letters to *The Times* on out-work and the effects of the Sweating system. She was also thinking hard about her future. Charles Booth suggested she should go on to make a study of women's work in the East End, and the eminent economist Alfred Marshall strongly supported Booth's idea. 'There is one thing that you and only you can do,' said Marshall when Beatrice visited him in Cambridge; 'an enquiry into that unknown field of female labour.'

Despite Beatrice's belief that 'every woman has a mission to other women – more especially to the women of her own class and circumstances', she did not take to the idea. She had other plans. Ever since her visit to Bacup she had wanted to study the Co-operative movement, for during her visit she had seen the value to the whole community of this public-spirited form of business, of a practical alternative to competition and acquisitiveness. Her friends tried to dissuade her. It was, they said, a man's world and unsuitable for her. She persisted. 'Still with that disagreeable masculine characteristic of a "persistent and well-defined purpose" I shall stick to my own way of climbing my own little tree.'

The rumours of Chamberlain's forthcoming marriage had proved to be true. Two months after the final breach with Beatrice in the summer of 1887 he had sailed for New York on a political mission; when he returned to England five months later, in March 1888, he was already engaged. The wedding took place on 15 November. Beatrice was still more vulnerable than she claimed. When she heard the news she felt it like 'a bit of cold steel in my heart'; and when Chamberlain's daughter wrote asking to see her she sent a friendly letter of refusal. 'I could not bear the pain of a re-opening of the wound.' It was a testing time: 'Oh it is hard to bear,' Beatrice wrote in her diary. She spent the afternoon on the eve of Chamberlain's marriage in Westminster Abbey. 'It is almost happiness to think that he is happy,' she thought. 'God Bless them.' Next day she woke at two in the morning thinking of their future. 'It must be over,' she wrote that afternoon, 'and they are man and wife.' Beatrice spent the next Sunday morning at St Paul's where she took Holy Communion. She had done her best to shut Chamberlain out of her life but at this moment her defences were not strong enough. After the wedding she collapsed into a week of nervous prostration.

All the same she was now better able to bear her sorrow; she had a strong will, tempered by the fires of the old passion and it helped her to face the New Year with courage and hopefulness. She noted that she was losing her bitterness, 'which at times has been very intense', and she started to pre-pare for her two-year study of Co-operation. It was hard going. 'March 7 1889: At present my strength seems worked out: it is with painful effort that I begin on Co-operation. I look at the detail to be mastered with positive repulsion, and I long every day more for the restfulness of an abiding love – and yet I cannot sacrifice work for which all the hor-rible suffering of six years has fitted me, and cannot forget the past.' Even now she found it hard to face life as a spinster. 'God knows celibacy is as painful to a woman (even from the physical standpoint) as it is to a man. It could not be more painful than it is to a woman.'

Beatrice had always been unconventional, and her close relationship with her father, who had come to treat her as an equal and as a business associate after her mother's death, had taught her to get on with men on their terms. Now her work brought her into a working world almost exclusively run by men, and she began travelling about the country to congresses and conventions, interviewing officials and sitting in on their meetings. It was a singular style of life, which puzzled her family and friends of her own class. One evening on a visit to her sister Lallie at Liverpool she appeared for dinner in a pretty black gown. 'While I was discussing vehement labour questions with Mr Cross, Lord Granville listened with a sort of puzzled air and when I, out of politeness, tried to bring him in, he looked still more utterly at sea, as if we had asked him to join us in conversing on Chinese metaphysics. What would a woman who really by night light looked quite pretty, want with such questions!'

The Co-operators and trade unionists with whom Beatrice worked found it equally hard to place her, but she had a knack for talking to them and they were astonishingly tolerant of her. One evening that spring when she had dinner with the Central Board of the Co-operative Union, Beatrice joined the group in smoking. This gave the conversation 'an air of business camaraderie', she wrote. 'I am a general favourite with these stout, hard-headed but true-hearted men and they look upon me as a strange apparition in their midst.' Of course, for all her professional reserve, there were some who saw her as an attractive young woman, and her interviews sometimes ended with unwelcome offers of marriage – 'this is the second one this year', she wrote in March. One suitor was Francis Edgeworth, Professor of Political Economy at King's College, London, but his dry academic manner bored her, and she began to despise herself whenever she felt like giving way to her emotions – 'that part of a woman's nature dies hard'. The reason for thinking of the matter at all, she decided, was *the supreme and instinctive longing to be a mother*.

With her mind made up against marriage, however, Beatrice now began to see herself in a different role, as 'the 19th century woman with her masculine interests and her womanly charm – womanly charm cultivated by her as an instrument of power in public life – in the movement of the masses'. Future generations, she thought, 'might see a Woman step out of the ranks as a Saviour of Humanity, a supreme incarnation of the Mother's instinctive wisdom for the welfare of her children and their descendants'. Yet despite this vision of a greater public role for women she did not support the developing campaign to give women the vote. She even gave her name to a manifesto opposing female suffrage. She herself was the personification of emancipation, a woman 'who clings to her cigarette if she does not clutch at her vote', but at that time in her life – she later regretted her opposition – she felt that women could play a better part in society if they remained outside the stresses and corruption of party politics.

In April 1889 the first volume of the Booth survey was published. It was a great success; in addition to leading articles in all the main newspapers, there was particular approval of the chapters which Beatrice had written on dock life and on the tailoring trade. Charles and Mary Booth were delighted by its reception and Beatrice, visiting them at Gracedieu, shared their pleasure.

Through the summer, which she spent at The Argoed, Beatrice gave herself to her work. She had developed a regular routine: 'tea at 6 o'clock, study from 6 to 8 o'clock. Notes and chat till 11; Father till lunch. Cigarette and bask in sun and siesta after lunch; 3.30 to 5.30 study. Then a delightful walk or ride; supper, cigarette with Father; saunter in the moonlight or starlight; to bed at 10 o'clock.' Despite such diversions Beatrice found her work 'a grind and no mistake. Six hours a day reading and note-taking from those endless volumes of *Co-op News*'. At the end of July she could not help but remember Chamberlain's visit of two years before – 'shall always consider this day as sacred: a sacrament of pain fitting me for a life of loneliness and work'. Mary Booth was distressed by Beatrice's state of mind and she wrote a sympathetic letter. 'I am sorry, dear, that the old thing still shows signs of its deep root. I don't like and can't manage to get to like the idea of a future of work for you,' she wrote. 'I mean a lonely future of nothing but work.... If it is so, darling, it can't be helped, but I think it is a pity.'

There were occasional breaks from this quiet routine of life; in June, Beatrice went to the Co-operative Congress at Ipswich, then on to visit friends in Cambridge and London. There were also political distractions. Back at The Argoed that summer Beatrice watched the dramatic events taking place in London, where a strike in the docks had ended in a victory for John Burns and Ben Tillett, the leaders of the 'New Unionism', which transformed the trade-union movement by bringing in the previously unorganized and unskilled labourers. Early in September, Beatrice went up to Dundee for the meeting of the Trades Union Congress which saw the militant New Unionists and the new socialists forming an alliance against the Old Guard trade-union leaders.

In October Beatrice and her father settled down at Box House, 'our new and our last home', wrote Beatrice. It was a pleasant square building with a wide verandah and a pretty garden on the edge of the village of Box in the Stroud valley, within a short stroll of Mary Playne's house at Longfords. As Richard Potter's health gradually deteriorated Beatrice had to draw on all her will-power and an almost mystical religious faith to keep up her spirits and to go on with her work. 'Without help from the great spirit of Truth and Love I cannot do it. I pray earnestly that the help may be given me and that my life may be a "living sacrifice" to the work that lies before me.' She began to treat work itself as a form of religious truth; the 'sublime unity' of Science, Art, Morality were to her a form of the eternal trinity of the Good, the Beautiful and the True, and she saw the scientific method as a means to achieving virtue and happiness in a well-ordered society.

In the course of the autumn months she realized that her outlook on politics was changing; her earlier study of economics had been followed by exposure to the seamy side of East End life, and then by experience of the Co-operative movement and trade unionism. 'I dimly see the tendency towards a socialist community in which there will be individual freedom and public property instead of class slavery and the private possession of the means of subsistence of the whole people,' she wrote in a decisive diary entry in January 1890. 'At last I am a Socialist!' She was surprised at herself: 'this is where observation and study have led me in spite of training and class bias'.

Socialism was still a novelty, although there were a number of small groups in London which were engaged in socialist propaganda, and attracting recruits from members of the middle class who were repelled by the commercial values of Victorian England and appalled by the poverty around them. The most genteel and intellectual of these groups was the Fabian Society, founded six years earlier, which was led by a group of clever young people – notably George Bernard Shaw, then a literary and music critic with a desire to make his mark as a writer, who had just edited a volume of *Fabian Essays*. Beatrice had read these essays when they came out in November and their cogent arguments had played some part in shaping her views.

When Beatrice went up to London at the beginning of January to stay with the Courtneys – at Christmas her sister Kate invited her as a change of scene to stay at Cheyne Walk, and she went with them to Robert Browning's funeral in Westminster Abbey – Beatrice found that the Fabians and their slim volume of essays were being much discussed in advanced circles. 'London is in a ferment,' she wrote, 'strikes are the order of the day. The socialists, led by a small band of able young men (Fabian Society) are manipulating London Radicals.'

Beatrice was stimulated by this fresh political climate. The Fabians, in particular, seemed to share her concern with poverty, her desire for a more rational and more moral social order, and her belief that Co-operation and trade unionism were useful means to this end. Eager to make headway with her work on Co-operation, she was looking for guidance on sources of useful material while she was in London. She asked Margaret Harkness for advice, and was offered an introduction to Sidney Webb, one of the authors of *Fabian Essays*, who was noted for his encyclopaedic knowledge and his mastery of political tactics. 'He knows everything,' Margaret Harkness said. 'When you go out for a walk with him he literally pours out information.' Beatrice had already heard of this prodigy from common acquaintances. And when she had read *Fabian Essays* she had singled out his contribution, telling a friend that 'by far the most significant and interesting essay is the one by Sidney Webb: he has the historic sense'. Now she was eager to see him for herself.

CHAPTER FIVE

The Ablest Man in England

SIDNEY WEBB had already heard of Beatrice Potter when
he met her in January 1890. He had declared that she was
'the only contributor with any literary talent' when he
reviewed the first volume of Booth's survey in the *Star* in
the spring of 1889; and he was so impressed with the proof
that one third of the people in the East End lived on the mar-
gin of subsistence that he gave a lecture on the book in
Bloomsbury Hall in May. Webb was already a committed
reformer. As a reasonable and well-ordered man – he had
once won a prize for 'proficiency, punctuality and regularity'
– he could not accept the economic chaos of Victorian
society. As a civil servant he believed in a bureaucratic solution – the machinery of government should be used to make
Britain a more efficient society. And as a philosopher he was
convinced that socialism was part of the scheme of things,
telling Alfred Marshall in February 1889 that 'the course of
social evolution is making us all Socialists against our will'.

For the past ten years he had been an active Radical in London politics and after joining the Fabian Society in 1885 he
had made it an effective force for education and propaganda.
He gave all his free time to this work, which he considered
more important than his professional job in the Civil Service.
He was not a good speaker, with his husky voice, rapid de-
livery and unimpressive bearing. 'I am not a man of action,'

he had told a friend in 1886, and even in his political activities he preferred to work behind the scenes like a civil servant. Yet in debate he was enormously effective. His arguments were so convincing and ingenious, he was so well-informed and so sincere that it was difficult to get the better of him. He was little more than twenty when Bernard Shaw heard him speak for the first time and decided that he was 'the ablest man in England'. Shaw was given to exaggeration, yet his description of Webb was convincing. 'He knew all about the subject of debate,' Shaw said; 'knew more than the lecturer; knew more than anybody present; had read everything that had been written on the subject; and remembered all the facts that bore on it. He used notes, ticked them off one by one, threw them away, and finished with a coolness and clearness that, to me in my then trembling state, seemed miraculous.'

Webb was truly clever; since 1883 he had held the post of resident clerk in the Colonial Office, a position of responsibility which he had reached by his own determination to raise himself from his respectable though humble origins. He was born on 13 July 1859 at 44 Cranbourne Street, just off Leicester Square in the heart of London. His mother, born Elizabeth Mary Stacey, was an orphan who had been brought up modestly by aunts in Essex; with money from a relative she had opened a hairdressing and millinery shop which provided a reasonable and regular income. She was an extremely capable woman, a strict Evangelical who was also wise and witty, with a remarkable memory, and she saw that her three children – Charles, Sidney and Ada – were properly educated and trained in good habits. His father, Charles Webb, came from an innkeeping family; one relative was a jockey who twice won the Derby. Charles Webb married into the business, looked after its accounts and picked up outside commissions by collecting debts and local taxes. His main interest, however, was in politics. He was a public-spirited man, a sergeant in the Volunteers, a Radical in politics and a supporter of John Stuart Mill in the Westminster constituency. As a diligent reader of newspapers and pamphlets he brought a lively political atmosphere into the home; there was certainly a good deal of argument. Sidney remembered it as 'a happy family; we have always been in the thick of the fight'. The combination of religion and politics made this ordinary, modest and respectable family a little different from the neighbours. The Webbs, indeed, had few friends and tended to keep themselves apart.

Elizabeth Webb, who had rather come down in the world, was ambitious for her children to do well in it. At first Charles and Sidney were sent to a middle-class academy in St Martin's Lane; then in 1872 Mrs Webb, with an eye to their future employment as commercial clerks, took the unusual and expensive step of sending her two sons to a school near Neuchâtel in Switzerland to learn French. After three months they went on to Wismar, on the Baltic coast of Germany, where they stayed for almost two years in the house of a Lutheran clergyman.

In 1875 Sidney returned to London to a clerical job in a colonial broker's office in Water Lane, but he was not interested in this commercial world and, determined to turn his extraordinary talents to good account, he spent his leisure time at evening classes. At the City of London College he studied French, German, mathematics and book-keeping for four years and he went on to study economics, history and geology at the Birkbeck Literary and Scientific Institute, passing all his examinations at the top of his class. In 1881 he took the entrance examination for the Civil Service and was appointed a clerk in the Inland Revenue. He disliked the work and thought he could do better, and a year later he sat for a much more difficult competition for a place in the Upper Division. He came second and was offered a post in the War Office. Since this did not appeal to him he decided to sit the examination again in the following year, and once again he came second, being beaten by a clever Oxford graduate named Sydney Olivier. They both accepted appointments in the Colonial Office, and became fast friends despite the social differences between them. For Olivier was the son of a clergyman of good family, and Webb was the epitome of the lower-class scholarship boy, rising by a combination of capacity and industry. By the middle of the 1880s he had won a string of prizes which came to the considerable sum of £450, and even after his entry into the Civil Service he went on working to improve himself, studying law and being called to the Bar in 1886.

It was understandable that such an intensely intellectual youth should spend his leisure in an intellectual milieu. He certainly found it easier to express his ideas than his emotions, and all through his life he was personally reticent; though he had suffered a couple of romantic attachments – Shaw said he came out in spots when he fell in love – he never had much success with women nor did he greatly care for their company. He preferred good talk and the stimulus of debate. At the office, especially during the evenings of late duty when the resident clerks sat up to wait for telegrams coming in from the corners of the Empire, he enjoyed chatting and playing chess with Sydney Olivier, who had similar political views to his own; and they were often joined by Olivier's friend Graham Wallas, another clergyman's son who had been at Oxford with Olivier and was now teaching at Highgate School in North London. Bernard Shaw, whom Sidney had known since 1880, often made a fourth of an evening, and the young men became known to their friends as The Four Musketeers.

London in the 1880s was full of clubs and coteries which offered congenial and improving ways to pass the time, and Sidney was familiar with a number of them. In 1879 he had joined the Zetetical Society, a high-sounding but small venture where anything 'affecting the interests of the human race' could be discussed, and it was here that he met Shaw, when the penniless Irishman was still trying to make a start in literature by writing novels. He and Shaw belonged to the

Dialectical Society, another high-minded philosophical group; and Shaw invited Webb to join the Land Reform Union, which was inspired by Henry George's *Progress and Poverty* to insist that the taxation of land was the basis of effective social reform. The Four Musketeers were also interested in economics, and they read the novel theories of Karl Marx in a French translation. Little more than a year after Marx died, and not very far from his Hampstead home, a well-to-do anarchist named Charlotte Wilson founded a Karl Marx Club to read through Marx's *Capital* and Webb, Shaw, Olivier and Wallas joined in meetings that were so lively that they would argue all the way home. Soon the club was given a more decorous name, and as the Hampstead Historic Society it served as a regular meeting place for discussions of socialist history and politics.

It was a time of reform, when many people were crying new worlds for old – in new scientific ideas, in esoteric cults, and secular societies, in movements for rational dress, vegetarianism and other forms of the Simple Life which served as a protest against the comfortable complacency of the Victorian middle classes. One of these fresh starts, the work of a small group of young idealists who came together in 1883 to discuss the notion of setting up a community inspired by spiritual rather than material values, was The Fellowship of the New Life. It barely survived, for in its first weeks more than half its scanty membership broke away to form a more practically-minded organization to which they gave the name of Fabian Society, a joking reference to the Roman consul Fabius Cunctator, who was supposed to have defeated Hannibal by his cautious tactics. Shaw joined the Fabians in May 1884, four months after the Society was founded. He recruited Webb and Olivier a year later, and Wallas – who was living in Germany for a short period – joined on his return to England in 1886.

The Fabian Society, which combined moral improvement with social reform, exactly suited Sidney Webb's temperament, and he soon came to share its leadership with Shaw—Webb's taste for grinding detail and his capacity for wearying work being a splendid complement to Shaw's gift as a propagandist of genius. With Olivier, Wallas, a journalist named Hubert Bland and Edward Pease, a young Quaker stockbroker who had helped to form the Society and became its secretary for many years, they controlled Fabian policy; even while they were still young people they were known as the Old Guard. They had no direct political ambitions; they were more interested in new ideas and in a programme of municipal reform – baths, tramways, schools, and libraries – which might be introduced on its merits by either of the main parties. The Fabian policy, unlike other contemporary forms of socialism, was gradualist, based upon the notion of persuading and manipulating professional politicians to implement the policies devised by the Fabian amateurs.

The Fabian Society kept Sidney busy and his reputation grew as he wrote tracts and newspaper articles and gave lectures to any organization which would grant him and other Fabians a hearing. Yet for all the comradeship of the little group neither Sidney nor his friends were truly happy. He had fallen in love in the summer of 1884 with a young lady called Annie Adams, and it was not until a year later that she rejected him in favour of marriage to a Liberal MP. This disappointment left Sidney depressed and he confided his feelings to Wallas, who was himself in a low state as his agnostic opinions had just obliged him to resign his post at Highgate School and to seek work in Germany. 'You are only in fashion in being in low spirits,' Webb wrote to Wallas in July 1885. 'It is odd that after having been pessimist by profession for at least 7 years I should not yet have exhausted all the shock of every new surprise and disappointment at finding the world an uncomfortable one.' Sidney went down to the West Country for a short holiday to recover his spirits. 'I think it's good to be alone sometimes,' he told Olivier. 'I felt almost happy in my thoughts on the way home and built all sorts of castles.' He also shared his troubles with Shaw. As an intellectual distraction he agreed to teach Shaw to read German, buying the second volume of Marx's *Capital* for the purpose. 'We shall find it very dull,' he told Shaw, 'in fact, I fear, quite unendurable. But we may as well begin it together, if you are in earnest about learning German.'

Sidney was in such a miserable state in August that summer – 'I am really very sick,' he told Shaw – that he decided to join Wallas in Germany. 'I have no repose of mind,' he complained to Wallas, 'but a self-devouring activity, which is very restless and impatient.' He thought a visit to Weimar where Wallas was staying might do him good. 'Why did God put such a thing into life?' he asked. Sidney was back from his holiday in October and the elections in November helped to distract him. 'I have settled down to a dead level of life,' he told Wallas at the end of November. 'I am much as I was 18 months ago, plus experience and several memories, and a certain unrest, and minus some of my youth and hope.'

Sidney was, however, a resilient person and although he was sometimes miserable, he could always use his driving power to work as a way of preventing his feelings getting the better of him. 'The momentum of existence,' he told Wallas, 'is certainly the most strongly optimistic ally possible.' He did his duty conscientiously, though without much interest; he worked hard at journalism and Fabian politics in his spare time; and he enjoyed the long holidays which his job enabled him to take. In 1886 he was up in Northumberland for a walking holiday on the Roman wall with Edward Pease who, dissatisfied with his job in the City, had taken up carpentry and gone to join a furniture co-operative in Newcastle. In 1887 Webb went on holiday to Norway with Charlotte Wilson and her husband. In 1888 Pease, still unsettled, decided to explore the possibilities of emigrating to America, and Sidney went with him. They visited New York, Chicago and Boston. Pease did not find any suitable work there as he had hoped, but his spirits had improved.

Joining Sidney on the boat at an Irish port, he announced his engagement to Marjorie Davidson, one of the intellectual young ladies who had attended the meetings of the Hampstead Historic Society. While Sidney was pleased at the happiness of his friend he was distressed that it would mar his friendship with Pease; he had lost so many of his friendships through marriage.

None of the Webb family was demonstratively affectionate, and though Sidney valued intimacy he did not easily show his feelings. All the same, Pease's engagement revived the pain of Sidney's own failed love affair and when he wrote Marjorie Davidson a congratulatory letter on his return from America in December 1888 he admitted that he felt lonely and unhappy; 'an old wound, which still embitters me, was torn open', he confided, 'and bled, as it bleeds now while I write these words'. He told her frankly of the loss to him of Pease's marriage – 'I am nearly thirty and during the last five years I have lost five intimate friends by marriage,' and he added that he felt despondent at his own inability to find a partner. 'I have often envied the ease with which others "catch on" to congenial spirits,' he told her, 'where I simply remain outside. I am of course very busy, somewhat serious, very analytic and introspective – but I hope passably honest, sincere, and not obviously hateful or repulsive. Yet I seem "left out" in more than one case and in more than one department of life.'

Politics was an absorbing distraction and Sidney made himself available to anyone who sought his help. 'I am rather great at vague knowledge of things in general,' he told Miss Davidson. 'Send me a line when you want to know anything and I will find out.' It was in this same spirit of helpfulness that he responded to Beatrice Potter's request for assistance. When he met her on 8 January 1890 in Margaret Harkness's lodging in Gower Street near the British Museum he wrote out, there and then, in his steady, round handwriting a list of manuscripts, autobiographies and pamphlets in the British

Museum which she might find useful. A few days later he followed it up with the latest Fabian pamphlet called *The Workers' Political Programme*.

Beatrice returned to London at the beginning of February. She saw Sidney again and they talked about Sweated Labour, and a few days later he called to give her a draft proposal for municipal inspection of industrial premises. Beatrice then invited him to dine with her at Devonshire House Hotel to meet the Booths. After this more leisurely encounter she confided to her diary her assessment of him.

Sidney Webb the socialist dined here to meet the Booths. A remarkable little man with a huge head on a very tiny body ... somewhat unkempt, spectacles and a bourgeois black coat shiny with wear; somewhat between a London card and a German professor. His pronunciation is cockney, his H's are shaky, his attitudes by no means elegant – with his thumbs fixed pugnaciously in a far from immaculate waistcoat, with his bulky head thrown back and his little body forward, he struts even when he stands, delivering himself with an extraordinary rapidity of thought and utterance and with an expression of inexhaustible self-complacency. But I like the man. There is a directness of speech – an open-mindedness and imaginative warm-heartedness which should carry him far.

Beatrice saw the Booths again soon after the dinner and after they had dismissed subjects like Sidney Webb, Sweating and other working topics, they settled down to talk about socialism as so many other intellectuals were doing during those months. Booth, who was sceptical, began by announcing: 'I have found a new definition of socialism; the prevention by a paternal state of the consequences of a man's action.' 'I don't agree with you one little bit, Charlie,' replied Beatrice, and they were soon launched on a friendly wrangle about the meaning of socialism. 'It was an evening of the old sort of triangular discussions,' said Beatrice. 'I have become a Socialist,' she wrote after the evening was over and after five pages of scrawl in her diary trying to get her ideas straight, 'not because I believe it would ameliorate the conditions of the masses (though I think it would do so) but because I believe that only under communal ownership of the means of production can you arrive at the most perfect form of individual development – at the greatest stimulus to individual effort; in other words complete Socialism is only consistent with absolute individualism. As such, some day, I shall stand on a barrel and preach it.'

Beatrice enjoyed her stay in London, caught up on the wave of socialist argument: 'it is curious how many persons wake up to the fact they have always been "Socialists"', she remarked. Going back for another look at *Fabian Essays* Beatrice found herself impressed by the 'delicious *positivism* of the authors, their optimistic conclusion that the world is most assuredly going their way, the plausible proof they bring in favour of their confidence, the good temper and the moderation – all impress the ordinary English reader.'

When Beatrice returned to Box House at the beginning of March she settled down to work on an article she was writing for the *Nineteenth Century* on the House of Lords Report on Sweating in which she tried to formulate her own remedies for the system – but after three weeks at it she was oppressed with a constant headache and felt 'sick to death with grappling with my subject'. She was thrown back once again into doubt and depression. 'Was I made for brain work?' she asked. 'Is any woman made for a purely intellectual life?' The presence of her sick father made matters worse as his condition slowly deteriorated. He now lay 'like a log in the bed' wanting only food, rubbing to relieve physical discomfort and reading to 'sooth the restlessness of his wandering mind'. Beatrice felt his presence 'like a black pall overhanging all things and deadening all thought and feeling. One longs for release and yet sickens at the thought of this weary desire for the death of one's Father.' She tried to decide what to do in the months ahead. It seemed best to postpone her work on Co-operation and settle down to six months' hard reading – 'the conditions here are perfect for study', she decided. She could not help noting how 'absolutely *alone* and *independent* my life has become'. All her agonizing suffering had turned her nature into steel – 'not the steel that kills but the surgeon's instrument that would save'.

At the end of April Beatrice invited Sidney Webb to visit her at Box for the day. She was so friendly and sympathetic that he told her the history of his life, how he had been educated and made his way, his thoughts and his ambitions. 'I have done everything I have intended to do,' he told her, and Beatrice made a note of their conversation in her diary. 'I have a belief in my own star.' Beatrice reacted against such self-satisfaction. 'Take care Mr Webb,' she said in a motherly tone, 'don't be complacent about small successes.' He was taken aback by her riposte. 'You reduced me to a pulp by your sympathy,' he declared, 'and then impressed your own view on me; you have made me feel horribly small – you have given me an altogether different sense of proportion – and yet I don't believe that I looked at things in a disproportionate way.' 'Come Mr Webb, you can feel you have humbled me – by making me a socialist.' And when he had gone she mused in her diary as to his future.

His tiny tadpole body, unhealthy skin, lack of manner, cockney pronunciation, poverty, are all against him. This self-complacent egotism, this disproportionate view of his own position is at once repulsive and ludicrous. On the other hand, looked at by the light of his personal history, it was inevitable. And he can learn; he is quick and sensitive and ready to adapt himself. If the opportunity comes, I think the man will appear. In the meantime he is an interesting study. A London retail tradesman with the aims of a Napoleon! a queer monstrosity to be justified only by success.

As far as Beatrice was concerned she saw him as a contact with the socialist party; 'one of the small body of men, with whom I may sooner or later throw in my lot for good and all'.

'I fear I cannot adequately convey to you the very deep impression my visit made upon me,' Sidney wrote on 30

April. 'I have thought a great deal about what you said,' he told her, 'but it was, after all, the manner of saying it, and the impression you aimed at conveying, which were of most importance. It was an act of frank friendliness as valuable as it is rare.' He told her something of his own state of mind. 'It is doubtful whether you are really more alone than it is possible to be in London.' He had decided that 'practical work is a partial corrective', and he went on to draw her into his plans.

I really must have a mentor outside the working circle, a looker-on who sees most of the game.... Another time, if you will allow me the chance, I should like to discuss with you the general plan of campaign, the arrangement of the long rolling fight all over the country into which the Fabian Society, and I in particular, am being more and more drawn.... We are, indeed, constantly seeking chances of translating the crude abstractions of the doctrinaire socialist into the language of practical politics. But it is difficult to know how to treat the Liberal leaders. They are generally such poor creatures, and so 'hopelessly out of it'. I wish their education could be taken in hand in some way that would save the Fabian Society from becoming more and more conceited. But, really, every day makes me inclined to say 'I told you so' over some event or another.

For all his reticence Sidney's letter clearly showed how much he had been impressed by Beatrice's sympathetic intelligence. 'Perhaps it may amuse you to know that I am revising my estimate of the feminine mind! Of course it is impertinent of me, but I *must* get to understand such an important factor in the world. (I hope women won't always resent being considered as "factors".) This is outwardly a conceited letter, but, indeed, I *am* humbled – much more seriously than you realise. Yours very truly Sidney Webb.'

Beatrice was quick to reply.

May 2.
Dear Mr Webb.

One line in answer to your letter, for I feel I owe you a confession. The 'frank friendliness' arose from a feeling of gratitude. It was in my first conversation with you last winter that it flashed across my mind that I was or ought to be a socialist – if I was true to the conclusions I had already reached; and by this sudden self-revelation you saved me months, perhaps years, of study. Thus I became interested in you and your work; and wished to add to it any little odds and ends of experience of human nature which I might possess.

When you have studied women, I think you will find this desire to be helpful is one secret of their influence. It is, I suppose, part of the mother's instinct, and joined with their intellectual dependence (a curious trait in even the most intellectual women) it leads to friendship between men and women – that subtle usefulness which will always make such friendships one of the greatest factors in life – so long as it is not blurred by the predominance of lower feeling – when I think it becomes a source of pure evil – whatever the relationship may be. So you see, I shall expect to be used. I shall venture to ask help from you if I need it.

Yours sincerely
Beatrice Potter

Beatrice had, very delicately and in a few words, constructed the frame of their relationship. In less than two weeks Sidney responded to her offer. 'Already I want some help,' he wrote on 14 May. He had been asked to write an article on the Reform of the Poor Law for the *Contemporary Review* 'as people are half beginning to believe what I say I want to be right'. Telling Beatrice that he now felt 'some of the responsibility of leadership!' he sent her a copy of what he had written, inviting her comment and criticism.

I wish I could talk this all over with you: because I *don't want* to do anything rash! I am so driven with work that I can't think or do my best – I can only produce what comes. And all the time I am thinking (with my other cerebral hemisphere) of the glorious English country as it seemed to me one day in April and of all the revelations of that 'new world which is the old' – and then behind it all I who *am* timid, and cursed with looking before and after, fear to hear the 'ground whirl of the perished leaves of hope'. (Did you credit me with knowing my Rossetti?)

But of all this at some more fitting season. Meanwhile will you kindly counsel me? (Alas I cannot *promise* to obey – I will however learn.)

Yours very truly
Sidney Webb.

Beatrice replied two days later.

Dear Mr Webb.

I have read your articles with care and interest – they read fair and right, but I have no knowledge of the subject.... The idea of giving pensions to all alike – and treating the aged as *pensioners* and not as paupers recommends itself to me. On the other hand I have a lingering prejudice against any form of equalisation of the rates which would slacken the tie between the person who pays the pound and the person who spends it. . . . But frankly I have no criticism to make on your actual plans – I realise fully that the only helpful suggestions can come from practical experience – and that is a minus quantity with me.

For all that I am not going to deny myself the pleasure of criticism!

Beatrice went on to urge Sidney to think less of public opinion, to have more confidence in himself, and to collect information from experts which could be worked up in the light of socialist principles. 'True leadership is needed now,' she told him: 'it is of the utmost importance that responsible Socialists shall not make a false step, should not begin at the wrong end.' She went on to encourage his friendship once more. 'But do not let the cavilling of this letter prevent you from writing frankly to me whenever you feel inclined – and telling me your *real* attitude towards things.'

Finally Beatrice told him of her plan to go up to Glasgow on 22 May to attend a Co-operative conference. 'I am anxious to keep in with the leading Co-operators in view of any future work. Do not you feel inclined to come too?' Sidney was quick to take up her offer and to travel to Glasgow in her company. He had already fallen in love with Beatrice.

CHAPTER SIX

A Working Compact

'A LONG journey up in third-class saloon,' Beatrice noted about the journey to Glasgow in the exquisite Whitsun weather of 1890; 'I in one of the two comfortable seats of the carriage, with S.W. squatted on a portmanteau by my side, and relays of working men friends lying at full length at my feet, discussing earnestly Trade Unions, Co-operation and Socialism.' There was much to discuss since the sudden rise of the Labour movement had thrown up new ideas and factions to support them – the older trade unionists and the solid Co-operators both being suspicious of socialists, while the socialists had abused in the past the traditional leaders as obstacles to progress. In these circumstances the old-fashioned trade-union leaders were somewhat surprised to see Sidney Webb in their midst. 'He is humbler than I have ever seen him before,' said one official, 'quite a different tone.' Sidney, in fact, had his mind elsewhere.

Beatrice had been so friendly and encouraging that as they wandered through the Glasgow streets that evening Sidney tried to tell her what he was feeling. It came as no surprise. Beatrice had felt from the beginning that he would fall in love with her. But he was upset when she coolly kept him at a distance, and next day he wrote her a desperate note.

You tortured me horribly last night by your intolerable 'super-iority'. Surely an affectation of heartlessness is as objectionable as an affectation of conceit. And you blasphemed horribly against what is highest and holiest in human relations. I could not speak my mind last night, but this agony is unendurable. I do not know how to face another night such I have passed. Come off somewhere and let us clear up what is more important than all Congresses.

They took another long walk that evening and as they made their way through the crowded streets of the grim Scottish city, jostled by drunken girls and the low life around them, gilded for once by a glorious sunset, they came to a working compact.

'You understand,' Beatrice told him, 'you promise me to realise that the chances are 100 to 1 that nothing follows but friendship. If you feel that it is weakening your life, that your work is less efficient for it, you will promise me to give it all up?'

'I promise you,' he said. 'However it ends I will make it serve my life – my work shall be both more vigorous and higher in tone for it. I will *make* you help me, and I will insist on helping you – our relationship shall be judged solely by the helpfulness to each other's work. Forgive me, if I say that I believe that if we were united we could do great things together – I will not bother you with that; but I will vow solemnly that even if after a time we part, I will do better things for our friendship than I could have done without it.'

'One word more,' Beatrice replied. 'Promise me not to let your mind dwell on the purely personal part of your feeling. I know how that feeling unfulfilled saps all the vigour out of a man's life. Promise me to deliberately turn your mind away from it – to think of me as a married woman, as the wife of your friend.'

'That I can hardly promise. But I will look at the whole question from the point of view of health : as you say I will not allow myself to dwell on it – I will suppress the purely personal feeling – I will divert my imagination to strengthen the working tie between us.'

Everything seemed to be settled. 'One grasp of the hand,' Beatrice recorded in her summary of the conversation, 'and we were soon in a warm discussion on some question of Economics.'

Their own compact was matched by the conciliatory tone of the Congress. Sidney, in the name of London socialists, apologized for the earlier taunts of militants and offered the hand of friendship. The effect was dramatic, Beatrice wrote as she assessed the new opportunities created by this agreement; 'the whole scene gave one the feeling that Socialists had hardly begun their propaganda'.

Back in London, where she had time to think of all that had happened, she felt anxious about the personal step she had taken. 'It is a very solemn thought to feel you have a man's soul in your keeping,' she mused. She went to Westminster Abbey and prayed she might be worthy of the trust – 'that it might raise my life and his to a higher level of Service'. One of the reasons that she held Sidney at such a distance was that, despite all that had happened, her heart was still locked in its attachment to Chamberlain. When the relationship with him had finally come to an end, she had collected and put away in a sealed envelope all the letters that had passed between them. Now, in an attempt to free herself, she broke the seal and looked again at the correspondence 'to try and rid my mind of the whole story by seeing the actual facts'. She had to confess that, for all her efforts, the relationship 'has haunted me day and night. I watch his life with feverish interest, tracing with a horrible ingenuity those qualities that pained me, undermining the public usefulness of his life – I observe narrowly from all the tiny details I can gather from newspaper paragraphs and personal gossip the effect of his marriage on his character.' She tried to look with dispassion on why it had all gone so wrong between them and she had to admit 'whatever may have been his faults towards me – there were ample in myself to account for all the sufferings I passed through. Can I be brave and sensible and once for all vow that I will forgive and forget?'

In this torn state of mind she was concerned that Sidney should not misunderstand the situation. Now she wrote to him setting out her position.

May 29.
Dear Mr Webb.

I lay awake last night feeling perplexed and miserable about all that had passed at Glasgow. Do not let us misunderstand each other. It is the first time in my life that I have granted friendship to a man who has desired something more. But the motive which has led me to depart from what I conceive to be the safe and honourable course has not been that I think there is any probability of a closer tie, but that I regard our work of greater importance than our happiness and that I feel the enormous help we may be to each other.... Now I almost fear ... that you hope and expect that it will lead to something more....

I want you to realise that you will be betraying my confidence and trust if you allow yourself to build up a hope.... Personal happiness to me is an utterly remote thing; and I am to that extent 'heartless' that I regard everything from the point of view of making my own and another's life serve the community more effectively....

But you are still young and have life before you; *you* can hope for happiness ... if your imagination were free you might find one who could give you the love of a young life – of a life which has not been forced through the fire and forged into a simple instrument for work.... If I find that our friendship leads to constant perplexity and anxiety on my side ... I shall retire absolutely and entirely from it....

Sidney replied the next day.

Dear Miss Potter.

Your letter is full of mistrust – mistrust of me, mistrust of the not-ourselves which makes for Righteousness, mistrust even of yourself.... It springs from your generosity to me, your fear lest you do me harm.... Whatever harm you can do to me, has been done already. I cannot be any deeper in the stream ... because I am

through and through yours already.... I do not pretend to be indifferent to personal happiness. I think you are wrong to make light
of it for yourself. You cannot be at your best without it.... Now
you are to me the Sun, the Source of all my work.... You are
making all things new to me. You are simply doubling my force.
But I must not in the least tie or fetter you ... nor must I pester
you with my feeling. We must have a more detailed Concordat.
On your part you must give me some chance of personal intercourse for the sake of our respective mental progress.... I shall be
very hungry but I can be very patient.... We will be together as
friends.... I will not seek to remind you that I am your slave
also.... I can be in love without any desire for possession....
Whether we are ever destined to be united or not, you are a source
of Life and Work and Happiness to me.... When I think how
much I am in your hands I am almost ashamed to have fallen so
low. But I could not have been or done otherwise. Now it is for
you to choose because I am absolutely in your power. *Be honest
with yourself*.... Do not sacrifice everything to your intellectual
work.... You would be making an idol unto yourself. Your altruism would become an egoism. You would lose your subtle sympathy.... You would have dried up 'warmheartedness' in order
to get Truth – and you would not even get Truth. Do not crush
out feeling. I would rather see another man successful than that
this worse thing should happen to you. I cannot believe that you
will commit this emotional suicide. I ask you to 'give me a chance'.
Will you simply let things alone and see what happens?

'Let it be as you say,' wrote Beatrice next day. 'I will not
withdraw my friendship unless you *force* me to do so, by
treating me otherwise than as a friend.... Your letter has
touched me deeply *but it must be the last word of personal feeling.*'

Sidney took her at her word and he devoted the letter he
wrote to her four days later to impersonal matters, particularly the article Beatrice had written on the reform of the
Sweating system. Although he thought it was of first-rate
quality, 'magnificently put together', he thought it 'a little
vague' in its practical proposals. 'There will be a Bill
introduced by the London Liberal members next session

on the subject, and we must consult together how this should be drafted. You rather shirk the dry ground of draft clauses.'

Beatrice received this long businesslike letter when she was on holiday in Austria. She had left England at the beginning of June for a holiday in Bavaria and the Dolomites where she went with a new friend, Alice Green, the Irish-born widow of the historian John Richard Green who had made a great reputation with his *Short History of the English People*. Stopping off along the way at Cologne, Beatrice recalled the two other occasions when she had knelt there at the Cathedral and she had prayed for help and guidance to be humble and pure. Now she had passed through the fire. 'But am I chastened?' she asked. She was 'still vain and self-ful', she admitted, and thought 'of the worship a man is giving me – not me – but Woman through me – and I prayed again that I might make my life a temple of purity wherein to receive it. And I, so vain, so impure – God help me.'

The two ladies whirled their way through the hot days revived by new scenes in one German town after another and then on to a restful stop in the Dolomites among the 'pinnacles and fortresses of grey and pink rock rising out against the blue blue sky'. The high point of the holiday was a visit to Oberammergau to see the Passion Play, and Beatrice took the opportunity of a day of wet weather to write about it to Sidney, urging him to go and see it; 'it is a vivid representation of the revolt of the workers and the women, led by a great socialist, from the tyranny and false conventions of the moneyed and official class – the cause betrayed by a profit sector!' She also commented on his criticism of her article on Sweating.

Yes: you are quite right; my paper is 'politically ineffective'.... I do not agree with *all* the details of your objections (we will talk them over when I come back to London) nor with *all* your suggestions – but then I feel I am not a good judge. Still less do I agree with your suggestion that I should meddle further in the matter.

Drafting clauses is not my *fach* in life.... I am totally unfitted to initiate and advocate special reforms.

Through the peaceful days of the holiday Beatrice's thoughts had continued to run on to her relationship with Sidney, and she again shared some of her fears with him.

Is there to be absolute freedom between us?... I have been brooding over the future of Socialism and the noblest way in which it can be brought about – and from that mighty thought I have drifted to considering the effectiveness of each individual socialist who is to leaven the whole.

I have been longing to warn you not to talk to people in general about the way in which you are edging your way into different organisations.... The general impression seems to be that you are manipulating – from that people argue that you are a manipulator and not perfectly sincere – and that you know and I know to be a false impression as well as a damaging one.... The introduction of the personal element – of self congratulation or of any other form of egotism – gives the impression that you are working for your own hand and advancing your own interests – and that your faith is a means and not an end. And all this to prove the expediency of unselfconscious humility ... of silence in all that concerns yourself.

You see, I am sensitive about the reputation of my friends – and desperately intent on their highest usefulness. You must be equally frank with me when you see a moral lapse or intellectual failure. The permanence and worth of a relationship depends on the consciousness in both partners that moral and intellectual growth arises out of it.... You ought to be very grateful for this letter – and value it as a mark of confidence. If the spirit moves you pray write and tell me all you are doing – regard me as a 'well' wherein to bury all you wish to rid your mind of ... relieve yourself of what is bad and strengthen yourself in what is good – that is the spiritual function of a woman, to be the passive agent bearing a man's life.

Sidney glowed with her interest, and her advice determined him to go to Oberammergau if possible. He replied to her letter on 16 June.

Dear Miss Potter.

I *am* very grateful for your letter.... You cannot realise how much it is to me. Blessings on that wet day! ... I am afraid I over-stated the criticism of your article. I was immensely impressed with its force and I was vexed that the ordinary politician did not at once accept it. But it has had an effect.... When you come back we will draft the Bill together....

Yes – you are quite right in your criticism of my egotistical loquacity. I must and will learn reticence.... Now tell me of other faults. Do you not realise that your real *fach* in life is to 'run' me? ... You could do so much for me if you will only have faith in your own instincts, and courage to cut out for yourself a new life, whatever the sisters might say. A very fearful responsibility has been laid upon us both – unexpectedly, undesiredly. We have the ideas which can deliver the world.... Shall we continue to count each for one or is there no way of making our forces count for eleven? You have it in your hands to make me in the noblest sense, great. I, even I, have it in my power to help your own par-ticular work. Let us, at any rate, walk reverently in the Garden of these Gods, the awful possibilities opening out before us. Let us humbly seek for the right course without regard to petty con-ventions or preconceived views as to our own lives. Between us two let there be at any rate perfect soul union. When you come back I have so much to tell you.

Such an enthusiastic response only made Beatrice chary and she sent Sidney a cautionary letter by return from Trento on 22 June.

Dear Mr Webb.

It is very hot – stifling – and I am foot sore and tired so you must not expect much ... part of your letter saddened me. You are expecting too much from me – if you do not take care – you will frighten me back into acquaintanceship! Remember we are simply friends – if you should assume or the world suspect more, the tie is broken, for good and all. Beware how you tread!

I shall be back on the evening of the 4th. Will you come and spend Saturday evening at Devonshire House Hotel – seven o'clock supper? We will go through all the things we have to talk over methodically. . . . You can rely that no word you tell me will escape. You can even use me as a safety valve for the personal note so that it may die down from lack of response. And you, on your side, must discourage it in me – in developing what is best, truest, in me you must discourage the love of personal power – it is degrading. Political life is horribly dangerous – so few natures come out of it untarnished – it tends so little to form social character with all its glare and glamour and the heat and dust of personal prominence.

Sidney in his reply on 24 June, again tried to reassure her.

Dear Miss Potter.

It was good of you to write at once. I did not hope for a letter so soon. . . . You cannot realise how much you have changed me. Do not let my happiness disquiet you. It gives me no claim on you and it enormously strengthens all the good elements in me. As to the future, let us wait. I have the most perfect confidence that you will do whatever is right for you to do at the moment when it is right for you to do it. Our ends are the same, our views are the same, our motives are the same. Surely out of so much identity there must come harmony.

I should like to go to Oberammergau for a fortnight but I cannot spare the time from my writing. . . . I am not over worked or exhausted – rather, curiously resilient, if there be such a word, and divinely intoxicated, the whole world seeming new to me, the very colours appearing in a new light.

While Beatrice was away Sidney had been reading about the life of Goethe, for whom Beatrice had expressed admiration, but, as he was at pains to tell her, he saw Goethe's life as an 'awful example of the result of pure intellect', a life of self-willed anarchism, an inability to work with others and a great deserter from the army of humanity. 'It is much harder to live *in* the world, doing its work, than on the heights of Parnassus or in the Convent.' But Goethe paid the price of his egotism. 'He thought to keep himself unspotted from the world and to do its work best by standing above it. . . . It is dangerous to try to be *more* than man, to be "too bright and good for human nature's daily food". . . . It is a

83

warning not to settle everything too confidently by pure intellect. We must recognise instinct and feeling as of some claim as motives. .... I feel myself sufficiently akin to Goethe (I don't mean in any conceited sense) to be able to profit by his example. I have already started to try. I shall be 31 in a fortnight: it is high time.'

Sidney's warning about Goethe did not stir Beatrice to break out of her emotional barricade. She was determined to keep her relationship with Sidney on a mystical plane. 'Self-indulgence and self-complacency must be fought against,' she told herself: 'these are my besetting sins and with an idolatrous friend may become more so.' She chose to believe that 'the worship is not of me, but of the Ideal for which I serve now as the chosen Temple.' And when her holiday was over she re-dedicated herself to months of strenuous work ahead 'enlightened by love and guarded by purity – body and soul a living sacrifice to Humanity'. On Sunday 27 July she took the sacrament at St Paul's.

Sidney, on the other hand, found it increasingly difficult to contain his own emotions. He had decided to take a holiday at the beginning of August and he saw as much of Beatrice as possible during July. They each visited friends in Surrey and on Saturday 26 July travelled back to London together. They met next day for lunch at St Paul's Tavern and spent the afternoon at Epping Forest. Sidney was full of enthusiasm for Alfred Marshall's large new *Principles of Economics* which he had been asked to review for the *Star*; it was his habit to read quickly, 'tearing the heart out of books' he told Beatrice, and now, being pressed for time in view of his impending holiday he read all its six hundred pages the evening of his return from the country. 'It is a great book,' he told Beatrice, 'but it will not make an epoch in Economics – Economics has still to be re-made. Who is to do it? Either you must help me to do it or I must help you!' He was eagerly optimistic, talking about economics and politics, and of a socialism which made spiritual inspiration the basis of good

Richard Potter

Laurencina Potter

Beatrice in 1863

Standish House, the home of the Potter family

Laurencina and Richard Potter with (l. to r.) Georgina, Mary, Maggie, Beatrice, Theresa and Blanche

Beatrice and Kate *c.* 1872

Eight of the Potter sisters (l. to r.), seated: Maggie, Kate, Beatrice, Mary and Georgina; standing: Rosie, Blanche and Lallie

Joseph Chamberlain in 1886

Beatrice in 1883

Unemployed rioters looting a wineshop in the West End on 8 February 1886

44 Cranbourne Street, the birthplace of Sidney Webb

me unhappy. I had
not realised before
that you will one day
probably be rich.
You had told me
that you had a small
independent income,
but I had not realised
that your father was
so rich. This is one
more barrier between
us — one more step
in that noble self-
-sacrifice which you

⑨

59

29/7/90

You were so "ravissante"
yesterday, and so
angel-good, that I had
all I could do not
to say good-bye in a
way which would have
broken our Concordat.
I had to rush away
from you speechless
to hold my own. Do
not punish me either
for the impulse or

A letter from Sidney to Beatrice

The opening page of an 1890 letter from Beatrice to Sidney,

P.S. Do not write that ...

Box House,
Minchinhampton,
Gloucestershire.
[? mid-end Dec.]
1890

Beatrice Potter and Sidney Webb at the time of their marriage in 1892.

works. As they lay and talked in the Forest Sidney read Keats and Rossetti to Beatrice and when they parted he could not help some words of personal feeling bursting from his lips. 'I give you leave to think of me,' Beatrice told him, 'when you would be thinking of yourself – but not when you have sufficient power to work. I have promised you – that you know is our compact.'

Before Sidney left for his holiday he sent Beatrice a note.

You were so *ravissante* yesterday, and so angel good, that I had all I could do not to say goodbye in a way which would have broken our Concordat. I had to rush away from you speechless to hold my own. Do not punish me either for the impulse or for my self-control. I have no lover's arts and if I had, the notion of deliberately planning to 'win' your favour is abhorrent to me. Be both as kind to me as you can, and as frank as you know how.... You were indeed angel good on Sunday but one thing made me unhappy. I had not realised before that you will one day probably be rich. This is one more barrier between us – one more step in that noble self-sacrifice which you must make to pick me up. I feel as if I could never ask you to make that sacrifice for me – just as I am. But I have never felt this exactly a personal matter. Upon my work, and your work, our relations must have a great influence. Frankly I do not see how I can go on without you. Do not now desert me. Do not despise me because I am at your feet. I feel it hard even to go further away from you.

Sidney's holiday took him to Germany with Bernard Shaw: they travelled to Frankfurt, Munich and then to Oberammergau for the Passion Play as Beatrice had suggested. While Shaw climbed a mountain above the village Sidney sent Beatrice a note about their travels. 'Shaw does not suspect my feeling for you,' he went on. 'He has even suggested that it would be a good thing for Wallas if you should favour him.' He also had second thoughts about the letter he had written to Beatrice before he left which, he admitted, had been written under strong emotion. 'I am calmer now in these hills, and feel how untrue it was. It was of course true in a sense, as expressing my present feelings, but even if you dismissed me abruptly, I should not die, and I intend firmly that I should not even spoil my life over it,' he told her. 'But you may decide quite freely and at your leisure – the time is obviously not yet,' he added. 'If more is not for me, I will ask for no more.'

The Passion Play itself had an 'overwhelming effect' on Sidney, though he and Shaw could only get cheap seats and they had to sit in the rain for six of the eight hours of the performance. Sidney told Beatrice that the actress playing Mary 'brought the tears into my eyes' but as a civil servant he confessed to some sympathy for Pontius Pilate. 'My profession made me realise entirely his position. I should have acted just as he did.' Unlike Beatrice, he did not see the play as a popular revolt. Sidney thought Christ and the Apostles too passive. 'The beauty of sacrifice qua sacrifice does not adequately appeal to me,' he wrote. 'The world needs work as well as renunciation, and though men need to learn renunciation (it is not only in love that we are selfish) women need perhaps to learn that they are much too docile, especially to men.'

Docility, however, was never a failing in Beatrice. When Sidney returned to England on 11 August he found a sharp letter waiting for him. Beatrice had criticized Chamberlain for his wilful arrogance; now she took Sidney to task for his words of dependence.

Dear Mr Webb.
I could not write to Oberammergau even if I wished (as the time allowed was not sufficient) and I did *not* wish, as frankness would have compelled me to write the letter of one who was hurt and offended with the form and the substance of your Tuesday epistle.... I ask you – is it delicate or honourable of you to use the relationship of friends, which I have granted you, as a ground for attack – for a constant and continuous pressing forward of wishes of your own which you know are distasteful to me – and which simply worry and distress, and rob me of all the help and

strength your friendship might give me?... The form and substance of that abominable letter seemed to me prompted, not by a desire to add to my present and future happiness, but simply by an uncontrolled drive to express your own feelings, relieve your own mind, and gain your own end. If it had not been the outcome of evident emotion – it could, really, have been a gross impertinence.... (One word more – you misunderstand me – I shall never be rich – only sufficiently well off to carry out my everyday life on the plan of greater efficiency possible to my very limited ability. That is all I care for.)

If you value the continuance of our friendship, exercise a little more self control – and occasionally think of me, and of my comfort – do not always be brooding on my effect on your own life and your own feelings. It is truly masculine! I do not quite know what the word Love conveys to a man's mind; but *that* is not what we women understand by Love – Love to us has in it some element of self-control and self-sacrifice. ... I have lent you Friendship – on trust – and it is for you to pay me back that before you seek to make me give you more. To think that all this paper, ink and thought should have been wasted on this vain repetition of conditions!... I am sick and weary of the question. Don't provoke me again. There now – I have done.

The last five days I have spent over Marshall's book on Economics.... Could we not read the book together?... My pony has just come to the door. Goodbye for the present.

Ever yours
Beatrice Potter.

Sidney wasted no time in sending a reply.

Dear Miss Potter.

I am this moment back from Germany.... Your letter has hit me very hard. Some of your blame I submit to: my feeling carried me away.... I have tried so simply to express my whole mind to you ... that your word 'impertinence' comes upon me rather as a shock.... If you only realised how much I have repressed you might perhaps not judge me so harshly. I will not offend again. You shall not need to write me another such letter: a terrible letter.

Yours truly
Sidney Webb.

Beatrice, meanwhile, had had second thoughts. She felt she had been too hard and before she received Sidney's reply she sent him a cool but friendly note.

I feel called upon to finish my letter to you, which I cut short, at the sound of my faithful Dormas ambling up to the front door.... Do you not think I am right in trying to master Marshall before I begin on the book? (which by the by is beginning to loom large.... I don't feel so strong for work as I ought to do after that long holiday). Would you like to set me a paper on Marshall's book and make me work out some new diagrams? In that case I shall be at your feet, and not you at mine, a wholesome reversal of the relationship – more in keeping with the relative dignity of Man and Woman ... which will relieve the one-sided strain of our relationship.

If I were your sister I should end up with three small pieces of advice. However old your coat may be (and that is of no importance) brush it. Take care of your voice pronunciation: it is the chief instrument of influence. Don't talk of 'when I am Prime Minister', it jars on sensitive ears. And be dutiful towards your friend and keep her up to the mark, intellectually and morally – feel your responsibility to correct and form her.

Ever yours
B. Potter.

Sidney now devoted himself to a long and considered reply.

This will be a long letter because I have much to say: I am going to sit up until I have finished it. Your very kind letter ... is appreciated – oh so much!... You may rely on my obedience to your signal that I go too far.... I do not think you can know how much you hurt me....

I wonder whether a woman adequately realises the dreadfully 'tearing' nature of a man's real love (or a man the 'wearing' nature of a woman's for that matter). I suppose I have a 'strong' nature, and go into this with the energy with which I go into other things....

You *must* study Marshall, but I would not wait to begin your book. I shall be delighted to read the book with you chapter by

chapter.... I don't think I could set a paper which would be useful
to you but we will see.... Let me say in conclusion that I am very
grateful indeed for your hints at the end of your letter. Please go
on, when any more occur to you. The 'Prime Minister' was a slip,
immediately deplored, a survival from the time when I took myself
less seriously, and really meant only as a metaphor. I have not done,
but I ought to go to bed, so Goodnight.

Sidney Webb.

How happy I am in writing this.

Beatrice had now overcome her annoyance and was glad
to reassure Sidney. She replied on 14 August.

I was glad to get your letter this morning. I had been pained at
the thought of paining you. Written words are desperate instru-
ments: one cannot modify or discontent them by look, voice, or
gesture.... This is not a letter – it is only a line to suggest that we
introduce regularity into our correspondence....

Remember that the details of your life interest me – your own
ideas and your relations to others – and the general progress of your
work of all kinds.

Beatrice was now in an altogether happier frame of mind.
'I feel so much stronger than I have done for years,' she told
Ella Pycroft. She had begun her book, she had friends down
to visit her, among them Graham Wallas: 'he is so perfectly
sincere and naively enthusiastic', she told Sidney and she
wrote in her diary that 'the charm is in the relations between
these men – the knot of Fabians who would run the world
– the genuine care for each other, the trustfulness and practical communism of property and ideas'.

She was also enjoying the countryside. 'I have come back
from the gorgeous theatrical Italian Tyrol ... to the quiet
greys, greens and browns, the long, low lying hills and the
sober harmonies of earth and sky of English landscape,' she
wrote to Sidney. 'Think of me rushing through the air on
my little cob; or wandering over the soft turf, in my bare
feet! What luxury one lives in! How can we reap all one

enjoys?' She was even able to write in her diary for the first time: 'I am very happy – hard at work – enjoying health – the lovely country – friendship.'

Sidney was not quite so content.

CHAPTER SEVEN

The Tie Stiffens

'I THINK I am writing to you today because I am unhappy,' Sidney told Beatrice on 26 August 1890. His disconsolate mood was touched off by his decision that he would not write a book on political economy as he had been planning to do and he saw it as a confession of failure. 'You had far better let your ideas simmer,' Beatrice had advised him; and this deflating suggestion had been accompanied by cautionary remarks on his long-term future. For Beatrice feared that his spare time might be swallowed up by routine political activity, that 'the whole substance of your brain will go into one form or another of propaganda or wire-pulling' neither of which 'can develop the very best qualities of character and intellect'. She thought it was more important to form 'noble character and *really* scientific views (the result of single high-minded research) than to score political successes'. In the few months that Beatrice had known Sidney she had repeatedly asserted her belief in his qualities and confirmed him in his far-reaching ambitions; at the same time speaking frankly and even condescendingly as his mentor, she had shaken his brash self-confidence – a characteristic that she felt bordered on self-conceit. Sidney found it difficult to cope with these ambivalent responses to his request for guidance.

Now I feel perplexed as to what I ought to do and vexed with myself because my future work is not clear to me.... I think you are partly responsible for this. You called me into consciousness of myself by believing in me and since then I have been much oppressed by responsibility. You must not imagine that I am reproaching you.... I am revealing to you the real weakness of self-doubt which lies at the bottom of my apparent self-reliance.

You see how much I need your constant help. I do *not* believe that by myself I can do much in the world. What worries me is the belief that I could do relatively a great deal if my life were properly dealt with and raised to its highest potentialities. I have seen a vision which is now never absent from my mind and to be content with anything less than that seems to me wickedness.

I suppose I am just now in the condition in which men exaggerate their own weakness, in being abnormally subject to the influence of someone else – and that is why to be in love without certainty brings with it so much pain. ... A man in love is weak, and 'to be weak is miserable'. But then, to quote George Eliot once more, it is what we would choose above all others.

I am not a little vexed by the way in which all the group work has lately tended to aggrandize me. This has certainly not been sought by me, and I have always striven to merge myself in the Fabian Society. Now that I have been pushed into a position of leadership, I feel, horribly, the responsibility of 'living up to it'. With all my belief in myself, I have really so much less than my friends' belief in me, that I am afraid.

You see how much I need companionship – not only for stimulus but for mental balance.

This is an egoistic letter, but you asked me what I was thinking about and there can be no doubt that I am thinking of how I can best live my own life....

Now all this is very 'morbid'.... But there can be no doubt that, just now, I *am* morbidly sensitive ... and you may as well have the true account of it. After all, common sense, and 'use and wont' ... reassert their sway, and so I shall simply go on writing despatches and articles, and lecturing, and organising and – waiting!
Sidney Webb.

'My hand is very weary with writing but I must send you a line,' Beatrice replied without preamble. They were now on such frank terms that they dropped the formal manner of beginning a letter, yet they were not so relaxed as to use Christian names. 'These times of depression and self-doubt sweep over one's work and life at intervals – they are hard to bear. All I would now say is this: my belief in you arose out of my faith in your sincerity of purpose – in the disinterested straightness of your aims. I have not estimated and do not care to estimate your *capacity* – so you cannot disappoint me in that.'

Although they met a number of times during the summer Beatrice kept Sidney at a distance. It was not the conventional distance of middle-class courtship. She had no hesitation about meeting him or travelling with him unchaperoned. It was an emotional barrier that she erected, sharply reproving him if he presumed to cross it. 'Do not forget all I said on Saturday – do not pain me by forcing me to repeat it. I see more of you so as to set our friendship on a healthy footing of a working intimacy . . . if I feel I am misunderstood I shall have no other course open to me but to retreat into permanent silence.' Sometimes they would spend the afternoon together. 'Shall we take some book with us?' Beatrice suggested. 'I want to understand Jevons Theory of Value and the mathematical method.... Would you bring your *Capital*: you might read it to me, if it be fine enough to get out to Battersea or some other park.'

In September they went together to Leeds to a meeting of the British Association where Alfred Marshall and Charles Booth were in charge of the economic section. It was this part of the proceedings which interested Beatrice and Sidney, and in the long debate Sidney made a 'rattling clever speech' which impressed Beatrice despite the embarrassment of his cocksure Cockney style. She noted afterwards that there was 'a great deal of conversation with my fixed companion', and they travelled back to London together by the late-night express 'indulging in the unwonted luxury of a first class, S.W. telling me the story of his examination triumphs and reading me to sleep with John Ball's dream. The tie

stiffening!' The William Morris romance of mediaeval frater-
nity had just the right elevating tone for the occasion. Back
in London, Beatrice noted that she was 'tired but happy'.

She was actually beginning to enjoy her friendship with
Sidney and to feel its benefits. As autumn drew on he again
went down to visit her at Box. 'I am very glad that you
enjoyed your short visit,' Beatrice wrote afterwards, adding
a cautionary reminder: 'I trust that after this we shall have
straight sailing in friendship without any deviation into sentiment. I have not the slightest doubt that we shall be useful
to one another as friends – and to me it will be a sincere
delight to hear good of you.' He was also becoming a man
of modest note in the world of Radical politics and a newspaper description of him reminded Beatrice of things that
had been written about Chamberlain ten years before.
'Strange fate,' she remarked.

Apart from occasional brief visits to London, Beatrice
spent the autumn months at Box and she began to make
headway with her book on Co-operation. She had a visit
from Ella Pycroft and they enjoyed outings in the Cotswolds
and to the edge of the Severn vale. Her thoughts, however,
were with Sidney and in her mellow frame of mind she sent
him a warm, encouraging letter: 'as the sun set and the effect
of sunlight, cloud, mountains, water and plain, became every
moment more magical, I *did* wish that you had been there
to share the intoxicating beauty, to heighten it by the consciousness of close human companionship – by the sense of
fellowship and worship as well as in work.'

She went on to tell him how their relationship now stood.

Let us go forward with this fellowship without thought for the
morrow. You are too generous and too wise to wish me to do
violence to my feelings – to wish me to *force* a growth which is
not natural. It is for you to win that dependence and respect out
of which the woman's love arises. You have already won the
desire to be helpful. You can feel as a stimulus, that whenever
you are less worthy than you might be you give me positive pain,

like the pain I felt when you were speaking at the British Association, like the pain I have felt when in general conversation you
have dwelt on yourself and ignored or disparaged the work of
others. On the other hand I am proud, very proud, of your
self-devotedness, of your disinteredness of aims.

I have been wondering whether you would change the form of
your weekly letter, whether you would jot down each day all of
interest you have done ... and send it me once a week? Though
I am absent you would then feel that I was by your side ... you
would enable me to feel part and parcel of your life, to watch it
and sympathise with it from afar off.

Now goodbye and God bless you. Think of me whenever you
feel troubled; don't overwork and look after the breadth of the
English vowel! Do not refuse to recognise the individual existence
of 'er', 'ir', 'ow', 'a', and confounded them all in a common 'er'.

Ever yours
Beatrice Potter.

Sidney was delighted to receive such 'a beautiful letter'.

Your suggestion is a very good one. I will try to think on paper
for you from day to day. First let me go back to your beautiful
letter. I think you will now believe me when I say that I do not
ask for more than you have given me – for more than this valued
friendship, and your help and counsel, *and* permission to wait
events. You will do the right thing at the right time and I am content to wait. I foresee that I am going to have enough to do this
autumn. No one shall say of me that politicians must not be allowed
to fall in love for it destroys all their effectiveness. I am quite sure
I have never done so much work or been so efficient as this glorious
summer. After all, happiness, like champagne, is of some use in the
world. . . . I have at last managed to get you a copy of Rossetti
– they seem to be scarce, and of course one can't get the much
nicer but presumably wicked Tauchnitz edition of the poems only.
This is the first gift I have ventured to make to you. Do you
know, I think I am too much in love to be a lover. My whole
feelings are so transformed that it does not occur to me to do the
ordinary things. If I lie awake at night and think about you, you
come in the guise of a co-worker – this is dreadfully unromantic
– though it is your own individual face that comes between the

lines of the despatches at the office. I *must* talk to you about this, because it is what I am always thinking about, willy-nilly, and because I may not confide in anyone else.

Sidney was always acutely sensitive to the lights and shades of Beatrice's opinion of him; and stimulated by her affection he was beginning to feel more cheerful. He was also encouraged by a boom in Fabianism that autumn. The cheap edition of *Fabian Essays*, still the only intellectual exposition of moderate socialism on the market, was selling fast, and the leading Fabians decided to take advantage of this wave of interest by an intensive speaking campaign in the north where interest in Socialism was spreading fast. Sidney decided to take some of his leave from the Colonial Office to give his share of the lectures, and at the end of September he went up to Lancashire to assist his comrades. Beatrice had suggested that he should keep a diary, and he began by noting his travels in little red penny notebooks which he sent off to her as he filled them.

September 21st. I am writing in Rochdale – the first morning I have ever spent in Lancashire. I got here at 7.30 after 5½ hours ride, and a very hasty lunch and ordered food. Before it was ready I noticed the advertisement of the lecture in the local paper as being for 7.45. It was then 8 so I had to leave the cooking food and run to the other end of Rochdale to hold forth at once, dinnerless. The lecture was therefore not good, but as it was only on 'The New Reform Bill' to an audience largely Socialist it was easy enough. After two of the Socialists – spinners – took me to a humble beer-house where I had supper and drank beer with a dozen gas stokers just off work, all virtually Socialists, who were immensely struck by the contrast between my hands and theirs as we clasped hands and sang the Marseillaise, from an English song book of which several had copies. There can be no doubt that our influence is just now growing very fast. Surely it would be well if our novelists were to emphasise more the *public* duties of life. Neither Dickens nor Thackeray, neither Tennyson nor Browning, ever thinks of man as a citizen. He is a lover, husband, father, friend – but never a voter or town councillor. We shall, in the future, have more and more to emphasise that the individual responsibility for life has to be exercised through the 'collective freedom' of democratic organisation.

September 22. I think Manchester streets make me unconsciously despondent. This Monday morning they are thronged with strangers and one realises what a huge job it is to impart even one new idea to these millions. How can John Stuart Mill fear that life will become uninteresting! To play on these millions of minds, to watch them slowly respond to an unseen stimulus, to guide their aspirations, often without their knowledge, all this, whether higher capacities or humble, is a big and endless game of chess, of ever extravagant excitement. I do not think I have forgotten for two hours together that it is your country.

September 24. I find this Campaign is very hard work, and I feel it telling on my nerves. This morning I feel ill-tempered and irritable. It is not so much the lecture every night as the irregular life: the perpetual talking to new people, the constant external stimulus. I feel dazed and unable to think.

Beatrice sent him an encouraging reply. 'Your little notebook was very acceptable,' she wrote.

But what extravagance of space leaving a whole inch and $\frac{1}{2}$ border – you might have sent me in this same little book 800 more words.... In the solitary hours of leisure I have been pondering over the possible simplification of life. We need to show by works as well as words that Socialism does not mean simply the grasping of good things by the 'Have-nots', but a deliberate giving up of luxury and fashion by the 'Haves'. Goodbye: I shall think of you during these evening lectures, and pray that you may appeal to good motive and use fair argument.

'Your letter raised me to Heaven,' Sidney replied,

and I have felt ever so much less despondent and so less bitter since I got it on Monday afternoon. What you say about Simplicity of Life is good and true. I have constantly felt that I was bound not to increase my personal expenditure, though my income rose. But do not sacrifice efficiency.... It is hopeless to try to express how much I feel. And I *am* grateful also.

Sidney.

Beatrice was now so well-disposed to Sidney and his circle that she made her own gestures of friendship. She had already been impressed by Wallas and he readily accepted her invitations to stay at Box House. Now she extended her hospitality to Edward Pease and Bernard Shaw but from Shaw she received a frosty reply. With characteristic bluntness he told her that it was 'the most unreasonable thing I ever heard of. Why, I find that it would cost me seventeen shillings for railway travelling alone; and where do you suppose that is to come from after an autumn during which the Fabian corvée has reached unprecedented proportions? I dare not think on what I have spent since the end of July without earning anything to make up for it. And now you, with the insouciance of a millionaire, calmly order me down to tell you about Lancashire.' Nor did he take kindly to such independent behaviour from a woman. 'No,' he went on: 'you may reduce the rest of the Fabian to slavery – they prattle from morning to night about Beatrice Potter in a way I despise – but if I am to go through my amusing conversational performances for you, you must come up to town: this lion is untameable.'

Sidney, on the other hand, was only too pleased to go down to the country and on his way back to London after an exhausting but encouraging tour, he made a detour in order to visit Beatrice at Box. She had already warned him to be discreet about their close relationship before her relatives and friends and on this occasion Beatrice was delighted by the modest way in which he behaved. Her friend, Alice Green, was also a guest and she took a liking to Sidney – 'a dear little man', she told Beatrice, 'one would get quite fond of him'. All in all, Beatrice was much more optimistic about him. 'He is certainly extraordinarily improved,' she admitted in her diary, 'and becoming a needful background to my working life – and I the same to him.' Indeed, 'the beauty of the friendship is that it stimulates the work of both'.

CHAPTER EIGHT

Blundering Devotion

BEATRICE went up to London early in October and she saw
Sidney again before he left for another round of lectures in
the north. She had been so friendly and encouraging during
the past few months that Sidney instinctively responded, and
behaved as though there was an intimate understanding
between them. In his enthusiasm, however, he went too far
in taking her for granted as his future wife. He misjudged
her friendly mood and she reacted sharply. Sidney was quite
confused by her contradictory behaviour. In an attempt to
explain herself Beatrice told him something of her earlier
passion – without mentioning Chamberlain by name – and
of its damaging effect on her emotions.

'Forgive me, it is I who am to blame,' Sidney wrote to
her after this painful encounter, and he went on to try to heal
the breach.

You had explicitly warned me that your kindness was only kindness
but you were *so* kind ... you threw me off my feet. Pray forgive
me. ... I know nothing of your story except ... what you have
told me. Dearest, it makes no difference to me, except for its evil
shadow on your memory. But do not let this memory cloud your
life or warp your judgement. ... I do not deny or conceal that I
am suffering very much this morning ... but I am not a child and
I have resolved that no such thing shall spoil my life or injure my
work. ... It is chiefly the thought of the pain to you and the shock

to our relationship which grieves me. .... I really can wait and I will not again be precipitate. You are right not to be bound. .... Dearest, I cannot pretend not to want you now – but I am strong enough to kill that want and forgo even your friendship and all hope if that is best for you. I do not think I am harming you, but you must decide. If you can let us go on as before ... it means so much to me. .... Do not take that from me – you have already changed my life – do not now cast it away.

Beatrice felt that she owed Sidney an honest explanation of her position, and she now wrote to tell him frankly how things stood.

Your letter made me feel very miserable; indeed I sat down and cried. But I will tell you with absolute frankness what I felt and have felt. When you spoke to me in Glasgow I did not say, as I have said to others, a distinct 'no' because I felt that your character and circumstances and your work offered me a sphere of usefulness and fellowship which I had no right to refuse offhand. I felt, too, how hard it would be for me to lead a lonely life without becoming hard and nervous and self-willed. On the other hand you were personally unattractive to me and I doubted whether I *could* bring myself to submit to a close relationship. Remember that I was desperately in love and for six years with another man – and that even now the wound is open.

Since then I have been trying hard to bring myself to care for you – some days I have felt the strength and calm which your affection has brought into my life. .... I have now a warm regard for you but I do not love you and until I do I will not be in any way bound. .... The question of marriage is not a practical one at present and may not be so for two or three years. My regard for you is not strong enough to face the terrible self-questionings of an engagement – the immediate pressure of the whole family. If I were in love it would be different – but I am not in love. .... Altogether I feel very very miserable. Try to forgive any pain I have given you, by the thought of my misery and also in gratitude for my honest effort to return your feeling. I cannot and *will* not be engaged to you. .... I should meet you, feel bound, feel it impossible and cut it once for all. .... Dear Sidney, I will try to love you, but do not be impatient.... What can I do more? I am doing more than I would for any other man, simply because you are a Socialist and I am a Socialist. That other man I loved but did not believe in; you I believe in but do not love. Will it end equally unhappily?

It seemed as if Sidney, like Chamberlain, had to be kept at a distance, although in each case there was a different reason. From early adolescence, as her diary reveals, Beatrice had been aware that men physically attracted her, but she was temperamentally afraid of them. It was from this conflict that her troubles sprang. She vacillated in her relationship with Chamberlain because, despite his sexual fascination, his personality seemed to threaten her survival as a person. She did not have the self-confidence which would enable her to cope with these paradoxical emotions. The situation with Sidney raised the same problem but she coped with it differently. From the outset she saw the relationship in intellectual terms, and was determined to keep it there – as if her independence could be best assured by an act of will. That was why she began by defining their association as 'a working compact' and continually reminded him of its conditions. Sidney, who wanted to behave naturally, was bewildered by such contrived behaviour. Although he patiently tried to understand, it made him nervous and he became increasingly frustrated.

Sidney was back in Lancashire when he replied to Beatrice on 8 October. 'This must be something like the feeling of the morning after an earthquake. I don't seem to know where I stand at all. ... Do not be afraid I shall make a mistake again – at least not *that* mistake. I shall have to leave you to propose to me, I believe.'

For all his feelings of embarrassment and frustration Sidney tried to look on the bright side. 'The sun is shining and I *will* write cheerfully,' he told Beatrice next day, 'though I sat and read Isaiah part of the night! (Did I tell you that on *the* worst night at Glasgow I read and reread Job? These Bibles in hotel bedrooms come in handy sometimes.)' In the circumstances, however, he found it hard to concentrate on his lectures and there were moments when he lost heart in his work. There were some sixty or seventy people at the meeting in Barnsley: 'it is entirely virgin soil and I *suppose* worth cultivating,' he wrote to Beatrice. 'I do not grudge the time and money,' he added, 'but it does sometimes seem much work for small results.' He could not take his mind off Beatrice and he read her letter again.

I am a pig to be discontented – you really give me all I ought to want. . . . What I need is your affection . . . the durable regard that comes from real sympathy and cordial trust. That you have given me, and do not think I am ungrateful. Then I want hope. That I have had from the first . . . chiefly from an inward knowledge and conviction that it *must* be, a tremendous belief in the reason-ableness of my proposal, of the transformation of I and I into II. . . . My conviction of its reasonableness is also a conviction that *you* will one day find it the same: but you will and must of course wait till then. I know perfectly well how little likely I am to be person-ally attractive to anyone; and I know also how all one's bad habits and tricks of manner are apt to be positively repellent. But if we two were alone in an enemy's country . . . all these personal details would sink into insignificance before our common aims and mutual sympathy.

Beatrice had also been unsettled by all that had occurred and a letter she sent to Sidney from Oxford on 10 October conveyed her depression.

I have just come in from looking over the town alone. . . . It is a glorious evening. Troops of undergraduates are arriving – the first day of term – and I took tea with a whole room full of them. For the most part they are seedy, common-looking characters. . . . I feel horribly sad – sad and hopeless about the future (not for myself for that I no longer care for) but of this young England with its poverty-stricken aims and its rampant animalism. That I suppose is an unhealthy observation – there is probably better stuff in them than in me if I could only see it.

Ever yours
B.P.

Sidney replied the next day.

Do not be despondent for the world. There is a great vitality in it – a 'will to live'.... My Manchester lecture was a great success. ... Things are obviously booming for us.... I fear that some big 'Labour battle' is at hand. The capitalists are becoming really alive to the situation and will try, as in Australia, to break the power of the unions.... Yet Morley and Asquith, Trevelyan and Labouchere, can find nothing to talk about but Ireland. The fact is they *don't like* Labour politics; they are uneasy about these new questions.

Sidney was doing all he could to see things in a cheerful light, drawing what comfort he could from any kind word from Beatrice. He arranged a party for a group of Fabian friends to bid farewell to Sydney Olivier, who was leaving for an official appointment in British Honduras and he was delighted when Beatrice agreed to come despite their differences. But he had been so thoroughly unnerved by her negative attitude that he did not know what to do with himself; even a hard grind at lecturing and journalism did little to relieve his anxiety. Back in London he could bear it no longer and in the quiet of a Sunday afternoon he sent Beatrice a letter in which he appealed directly to her sympathy.

I am alone in the house and (I confess) not very happy. I am weary and anxious and unable to work. ... It is unreasonable of me to want you to be here, but I do want you badly. This morning I lectured on 'Lessons from America' to the Upholsterers Club ... but it does not come to much. Now I am writing two articles for the *Financial Reformer* ... but I don't want to do them, I don't. But then I don't know what else I should prefer to do here alone, except go on writing to you.... Be careful with me just now, for I am evidently 'sore all over' and you may hurt me more than you know.... I *feel* very unfortunate because I can't get what I want here and now....

When I think how I should suffer if ... you did not want to see or hear from me again I can't help trembling. You have me entirely in your hands. As you are strong, be merciful....

I foresaw from the first that it would be so. I remember thinking that you would be likely to find my blundering devotion oppressive.... Dearest, I have love enough for two – you cannot *help* reflecting back love for me because my heart is so strong. Turn but your face towards me, and love must come – do but give up looking backward.... You must resolutely live for the future instead of in the past. Every time you think of your past sufferings you commit a sin against that world for whom you wish to live, you tend to harden your nature and dry up your feelings.... I am sure you need to warm yourself at some 'fire of life' and I may serve to save you from the growing numbness of emotional death....

Today my yearning is all powerful in me and I cannot see anything but your face. Do you remember Rossetti:

> O love, my love! if I no more should see
> Thyself, nor on the earth the shadow of thee
> Nor image of thine eyes in any spring.
> How then should sound upon Life's darkening slope
> The ground whirl of the perished leaves of Hope
> The wind of Death's imperishable wing!

No sooner had Sidney sent this letter than he felt ashamed and anxious about expressing himself so freely. 'I don't want you to do what I desire, out of mere pity and generosity,' he explained to Beatrice two days later. 'Besides it is not so bad as all that. There is no doubt that I had a bad week, having been "knocked over" (through my own blunder) in an absolutely unprecedented way. But I have "got into my stride again" now,' he assured her; 'it was a relief to write to you and I wrote just what I thought, without enough thinking how it might affect you.'

As he had suspected Beatrice was quick to react to such confidences; they only made her feel more miserable than ever and she replied in tones of annoyance mixed with despair.

Your Sunday letter made me feel very wretched – do not write like that again – do not 'let yourself go' – it is not fair on me nor wise for yourself. Remember your promise that no woman should spoil your life. ... I am feeling low and miserable – as if a great burden were laid on me – the burden of unreturned affection – affection which I feel it is unlikely I shall ever return. But it is our work that is important and not ourselves – in face of all the misery and senseless stupor of the world – we must not think of ourselves. You were over-tired on Sunday – so I do not blame – but do not repeat it – lest you make the burden intolerable.

Ever yours
B. Potter.

'You will have seen from mine of yesterday that I anticipated your strictures,' Sidney replied, 'so I cannot complain of them.' A more assertive note, however, began to creep into his correspondence.

But remember that I have had rather an unprecedented trial.... Indeed I don't wish to importune you: I understand quite well the position.... Only be careful for it is not a light thing with me. I don't want you to feel it necessary always to be entrenching yourself behind declarations adverse to me, as warnings to me. They don't really alter the situation either way. ... Don't say too much about our *work*: if it were to be decided on that ground alone there could be no doubt as to the answer....

S.

For all their troubles Beatrice came to London for Sidney's party as she had promised. He found it hard to dissemble in front of his guests about his relationship to Beatrice and, to protect himself, he scarcely said a word to her all the evening. She, however, made a good impression with his friends. The journalist H. W. Massingham, the assistant editor of the *Star*, spoke enthusiastically about her, and Sidney's friend B. F. Costelloe said how agreeably surprised he was to find her so changed since they had last met; 'now you had a new light in your eyes and an altogether different character,' Sidney reported to her.

During this visit to London Beatrice had dinner with the

Booths and they raised the question of her relationship to Sidney. The matter arose because they had invited Sidney a few days earlier and as the long evening's talk ranged over the Poor Law, socialism and similar topics, Sidney had sensed that he might not be making a good impression. He differed with Mrs Booth about the writing of history and with Charles Booth about the justification for socialism. 'I am sorry I failed to ingratiate myself more – if I did fail – but I cannot be other than myself,' he told Beatrice; and although he felt that Booth would not consciously resent his assertive manner 'it can hardly fail to affect unconsciously his view of me.' Sidney was right in his conjectures, for when Beatrice saw the Booths afterwards Charles told her that 'he is not enough of a man: you would outgrow him'.

The reaction of these close friends did nothing to dispel her own doubts; nor did the advice of her friend Arabella Fisher whom she had met at San Remo years before. Beatrice had already confided in Mrs Fisher in June who had then told her: 'If your affections are not engaged and you wish to stop you must stop soon as you say. Your relationship as it is must give him hope.' Now she spoke more firmly: 'I am afraid of your becoming entangled in a well of Socialism. I should not be afraid if the sphere of the man were of wider culture and a calmer more statesman-like mind.'

In this uncertain state of things nothing could be settled; all that Beatrice and Sidney could do was to press ahead with their work. Sidney was now in great demand. There were requests for him to write articles, make speeches and write books. The Liberal Party wanted to publish some of his articles and he agreed to edit them into a pamphlet: 'my policy is to be the future Liberal policy', he cockily insisted. He lectured in Wandsworth Town Hall to the local Liberal Association on the Eight Hours Bill, actively sponsored by the Fabians; 'I feel no doubt,' he told Beatrice, 'that we shall be able to drive the official Liberals on into a sea of Socialism before they know where they are.' For all the difficulties he was facing he was convinced that his tactics would be equally successful in winning Beatrice. 'You know my very certain faith on this point,' he told her, 'not always, I must add, a *serene* faith, yet even "when my light is low" a very real and abiding faith that it *must* be so – the "fitness of things" so absolutely requires and compels it.'

At the beginning of November, Beatrice went up to Manchester to pursue her research on Co-operation. Although she still remembered that 15 November was the day of Chamberlain's marriage she now felt that the 'terrible pain is like a passed dream: and even the scar is well nigh imperceptible – has the whole skin hardened?' she mused to herself. She began to conclude that she had fully recovered when she had a visit from Richard Burdon Haldane one Sunday at the beginning of December. He was a young barrister who had been elected to Parliament in 1885 and was now one of the leading Radicals in the Liberal Party. One purpose of his visit was to discuss an alliance between the left-wing Liberals and the Fabian Socialists; and as Graham Wallas had been visiting Beatrice at Box four days earlier she was well briefed. Haldane, however, had another purpose – an 'arrière pensée' of a suitable wife, Beatrice wrote in her diary. Her reaction was unequivocal: 'Ah! Mr Haldane: I will let you into a secret of woman's unmarried life: in my days of deep depression I brood over matrimony – but it is as an alternative to suicide.'

It was for Beatrice a moment of truth, in which she realized that it was not so much Sidney to whom she objected as marriage itself. 'I cannot bring myself to face an act of *felo de se* for a speculation in personal happiness,' she wrote in her diary; 'though I am susceptible to the charm of being loved I am not capable of loving. Personal passion has burnt itself out and what little personal feeling still exists haunts the memory of that other man.' She turned with increasing determination to her faith in her work, attending a meeting of dockers, and then going up to Leicester in bitterly cold weather to a Co-operative Society meeting. On this occasion she was called on to speak but she was too nervous to do it well. 'It will be a long time before I am fit for much in public speaking,' she concluded.

Sidney was still uncertain how matters stood. Then, at the end of November, he went down with scarlet fever. He was annoyed at being seriously ill and house-bound; for a few days he could not write, and even when he began to mend he had to wait until the doctor agreed that a fumigated letter would carry no risk of infection. In his impatience and frustration, the self-abasement of his previous letters to Beatrice gave way to self-defence. 'You have been good to write to me,' he wrote on 30 November, 'but you are always "hard" on me and you have contrived to make your letters bitter as well as sweet.' He went on:

I do not deserve your scorn about impatience, scorn really of man not of me. . . . Dearest, you know I *want* you to be my critic and I do not resent it even when I think it forgetful of the 'extenuating circumstances' which I plead in return. But do not attack me as a representative of Man. You have an undercurrent of 'anti-male' feeling. . . . I think the 'subjection of woman' is bringing as its Nemesis a growing anti-male tension. . . . It would be an evil thing if women formed a huge trades union or protective confederacy against men. I don't want the next great war to be, as Henry James half seriously predicts, between the men and the women. . . . I *have* thought about my life a little but the thoughts were so bitter and so despondent that I have tried sometimes to banish them. I shall come back much humbled, and much less hopeful. . . . I think you are the cause of part and I will talk it over with you.

I have a new skin, but not a new heart and I find no hesitation or doubt as to my aim in life or my love for you. . . .

Sid.

He had hoped to be able to see Beatrice on 5 December but he was not well enough. 'I am told that I should endanger my life if I went straight from this room into the present weather,' he wrote. Such frustration and the depression of the illness made him all the more desperate. And his sense of crisis led him to bring his relationship with Beatrice to a head.

I feel that this is a crisis in my life, and I beg you to be patient. ... I must write what I have been thinking with infinite bitterness during these days and nights of sickness.... Six months ago I thought it probable that I should leave the Civil Service and carve out a way of public service in some more honored sphere. I no longer think it *probable* ... and expect to remain all my days a clerk in the Colonial Office.

Why do I trouble you with this? Partly because you were the main cause of my changing my expectations; you by believing in me made me believe in myself.... I see that I must forgo the hope of your one day consenting to marry me.... I realise how *impossible* it would be for you to fly in the face of your whole family to marry me. I could not, in decency, press you to do it.... Of course it would be easy if you loved me, but you have let me see only too clearly that you don't.... I confess I don't understand you.

I write this in the utmost bitterness of soul.... I need hardly say that I still love you with all my strength ... but if you are *quite* sure that no advantage to your own life or mine, or to the Socialist cause, could ever induce you to marry me, then it is your duty to tell me so and I must bear it how I can....

S.

In his anger he destroyed the letters which Beatrice had recently sent him. There was, however, no relief or comfort in the letter which Beatrice now wrote.

I cried very bitterly over your letter and tossed about the night through feeling how wrong it had been of me to have been led away from my better judgment last spring and to have granted your request for friendship. But that is now done – and cannot be undone – the question is what is the present position?

First, all you write about your career does not affect the one question. It would suit my work – and therefore me – far better to marry a clerk in the Colonial Office than a leading politician to whose career I should have in the end to sacrifice my own. It was exactly your position which made me hesitate – it was this with

109

your views and your moral refinement which made me try to love you.

But I do not love you. All the misery of this relationship arises from this ... there is no change in my feeling except a growing certainty that I cannot love you.

To be perfectly frank I did at one time *fancy* I was beginning to care for you – but I was awakened to the truth by your claiming me as your future wife – then I felt – that what I cared for was not *you* but simply the fact of being loved....

Frankly, I do not believe my nature is capable of love. I came out of that six years agony ... like a bit of steel. I was not broken but hardened – the fire must do one or the other. And this being the case – the fact that I do not love you – I cannot, and will never, make the stupendous sacrifice of marriage....

This makes it absolutely necessary that our present relationship should be ended: we must be absolutely firm.

Do not fail in the crisis of your life – do not be disheartened because the immediate road to personal happiness is closed to you. Think of your life and of your health and strength as not yours to give away or to fritter but as belonging to the cause to which we are both ably devoted.

Ever yours
B.P.

It seemed as if a decision had at last been made. Sidney, no longer desperate and angry, took the blow calmly.

I cannot resist writing to you immediately, though I feel very bitterly that my letters have undone me.

I want to assure you that I feel no anger, no bitterness against you. Your letter is an honourable and worthy one, and I am surprised to find that I am convinced that you have decided aright....

And I accept your decision. You will not find that I have ceased to love you, but I will cease to regard you as a 'marriageable' person.

If I adhere to that, do not let us cease to be friends, and intimate friends....

The *loneliness* of life! What a 'long unlovely street' it seems. Pray let us continue friends for I feel I have literally no one else....

Au revoir.
Sidney Webb.

Beatrice felt 'cold at heart' at what she had done and she tried to soften the blow by following up her letter with a kindlier note.

Dear Mr Webb.

I want to add one word more to my letter of Sunday.

You are not alone in your suffering. I have suffered acutely this last week – indeed ever since I felt that I must no longer mislead you. I suffer from knowing of your suffering and also from a sense of the terrific 'loneliness'....

God bless you: I would give a good deal to have it all undone – all I can do now is to insist on the past being wiped out, or broken with.

Ever yours sincerely
B.P.

Nevertheless Beatrice stood by her decision. She was now in Leicester and while she was there she sent Sidney a kind but firm note, laying down a strict set of rules as conditions of friendship as if it were a legal contract.

Dear Mr Webb.

Your letter of Saturday is quite worthy of you and the trust I laid on you when I granted your request last spring. You promised me then that you accepted the intimate friendship with all its risks and that you would abide by my final desire....

Now about the future. I cannot honourably allow you (at least for the present) to be my intimate friend; and personally, I think it would be far better for you that we should see nothing of each other and that I should even sever my acquaintance with your immediate friends.... But I am willing to remain on friendly (tho' not intimate) terms on these conditions.

1. That any correspondence between us should be so worded that it might be read by anybody....

2. That all the letters written by either to the other up to the

III

end of this year should be returned to the writer thereof in a sealed packet; and that the sender should declare that none have been retained.

3. That I should receive from you, with my letters, a solemn promise that you will break off the friendship if you find it is leading again to hopes and that on no possible contingency will you reproach me ... for having misled you....

Think all this over: do not write to me for another week or so. ... The conditions I have given you are the 'minimum' and must not be disputed.... I should consider any refusal of these conditions as a way of telling me that you thought as I did – that the whole thing should be broken. I write from my bed: I have been poorly and out of sorts lately – and hotel life in bitter cold weather is not invigorating.

Yours sincerely
Beatrice Potter.

PS Do not think me hard. I am thinking more of you than of myself.

Sidney was now down in Bournemouth where he was convalescing and Wallas joined him there for walks in the cold bright weather. Gradually Sidney recovered his strength and morale: 'you certainly need not reproach yourself with anything as far as I am concerned,' he assured Beatrice.

I think I have recovered. I am certainly not unhappy, and not in the least 'tearing my hair' or pining away.... I do not think I am one to let the inevitable trouble me long....

Now I come to your question, are we to be friends or strangers?... I think you are in duty bound to join the Fabian Society, to act with us and to lend your counsel in public affairs to those with whom you agree. It would be wicked of you to withdraw your friendship with Wallas, for instance.... Those same considerations compel us, I think, to be friends....

Of course you are quite right to impose conditions: I quite agree to them all....

Do not refuse to continue to correspond....

I do not see why we should not be 'intimate' friends but that will be as you please....

The friendship between a man and a woman of like sympathies can be a very beautiful thing: of infinite use and joy to both of

112

them.... I see no reason why it need preclude or hinder either you or me falling in love and marrying elsewhere, if this be our destiny....

Dearest, I can never again write to you without reserve. Let me say what I feel tonight without disguise. I sincerely *hope* for your sake and for the world, that it may come to you to marry.... I am afraid for you. It seems very difficult for a woman to go on leading a lonely life, without wifehood or motherhood, without unconsciously losing much of 'warmheartedness' without sinking into sourness and narrowness.... 'Great thoughts come from the heart' – and the heart needs *nourishing*....

Next time I must write only as a friend. But *be* my friend as you well know how, and I shall learn gradually to cease to regret that you would be no more.

Sidney Webb.

When Sidney returned to London at the end of December he sent back Beatrice's letters.

I suggest that you should not read them – not that there is anything with which you need reproach yourself, but because there would be no utility in your realising the feelings with which I have put together these memorials of a summer. You are not cruel and I know that you feel yourself every turn of the screw of my torture....

I have taken for my motto '*Be Patient*' – that is what your initials shall mean to me.

Sidney Webb.

Beatrice was touched by Sidney's dignified attitude. 'He has behaved nobly,' she wrote in her diary. But she did not relent. 'Your letter is very noble in tone,' she told him, 'but you will of course remember that in future you must write as a friend, as a friend only.'

As the year closed she summed up her feelings in her diary. 'A year of Love,' she wrote, 'accepted but not given. The tie that was tightening between me and another, I have snapped asunder and I am alone again, facing work and the world.'

113

CHAPTER NINE

The World Will Wonder

'MY thirty-third birthday!' Beatrice wrote in her diary on 22 January 1891. 'Working hard and working well.' She was back in the routine at Box House, caring for her dying father and making progress with her book on Co-operation. She was content: 'in spite of my thirty-three years,' she wrote, 'I feel younger than I have ever done before: except that I feel horribly "independent", absolute mistress of myself and my circumstances – uncannily so. "Men may come and men may go but I go on forever."'

Sidney was in a very different state. When Beatrice went up to London at the beginning of January and met Sidney with Wallas, she saw that he was 'weak and miserable: not strong enough to work – and excited and jealous – more deeply involved than ever', and she began to wonder whether it would even be possible for her to continue 'honourably as S.W.'s friend'. Even minor matters had become a source of strain. Beatrice had already talked to Sidney and Wallas about joining the Fabian Society, but she was worried 'lest it should injure my chances as an investigator'. Then she changed her mind and gave way to the extent of sending an anonymous subscription. 'I wish I were *absolutely convinced*,' she confessed to Sidney. 'I am not yet. Every now and then I am haunted by a fear of waking up from a dream: my individualist antecedents have still a hold on me.'

Sidney reacted with unusual irritation, feeling that she had deceived him about her political dedication as well as her personal commitment to their relationship. 'I did not know you were still in the stage of doubts,' he told her on 19 January. He was still concerned, too, at the way in which she was living an isolated and possibly demoralizing life – 'taking up a position full of subtle moral danger', and he dreaded 'that horrible intellectual coldness which unconsciously grows upon the student'. He begged her not to 'sacrifice action to thought, for you would then, gradually and quite unconsciously to yourself, cease to get even thought'.

As for himself, Sidney admitted that he was finding it hard to cope with life. 'The fever has been a turning point in my life in more ways than one, and I don't feel sure which way I am going. I have got to stand alone, but whether I can do so is not certain. What potentialities there were in me before, are no longer there. . . . But I don't know that anyone could help me, even if anyone cared to do so. I only know that I am seriously in need of help.' To keep himself busy he turned his mind to writing a history of the Eight Hours movement in collaboration with Harold Cox, a politically-minded lawyer, but that did not resolve the problem of his professional and personal future. He grew impatient with his friends, argumentative and irritable in political discussions. On 27 January he confided his difficulties to Beatrice.

I am perplexed about my own life. I *like* to stay on at the CO but I feel every day more that I am shirking the tasks of life in so doing. The need for *someone* in Parliament is very great. . . . The need for new men in the County Council in November next is also very great, and I could virtually ensure a seat there at once. This makes it clearer to me that I ought to give up the CO in the autumn; go into the County Council election in November (which I cannot do without resigning here) . . . and throw myself boldly upon the world, to earn my living by journalism and possible scraps of practice at the bar. Twelve years of official life have already so far corrupted me that I am afraid. I distrust my power to earn money;

I distrust my physical endurance; I am fearful lest my brain should break down; I dislike and shrink from the publicity, the electoral campaigns and so on. . . .

If I only knew what I *ought* to do. . . .

Is there nothing I can do for you? Do not make our friendship one-sided.

Sidney Webb.

Beatrice sent a sympathetic but formal reply.

Dear Mr Webb.

I can fully realise how it must be troubling you to come to any decision; and I know too little about the chances of life to give you any assistance.

Personally . . . I do not think that with your strong convictions and your desire to help things forward you will be satisfied without throwing yourself into the stream. . . .

I think you are admirably suited to Parliamentary and Administrative life, and the LCC would be splendid training. 'Publicity' is not a thing that any citizen ought to shrink from . . . Can you make a sufficiently liberal income in journalism to allow you to do Public Work over and above Pot-boiling? . . .

Ever yours sincerely
Beatrice Potter.

Only in a postscript did she give way to a personal note when she added: 'I have a splitting headache, I suppose it is the sultry weather.'

It was almost a month later that Sidney wrote to say that he was now quite well but he had still not decided what to do about his career, 'but it is more and more plain to me what I ought to do, and I hope I shall have courage enough to do it. . . . Meanwhile I am making known that I am for sale, and perhaps some good and well-paid work may come along.'

He chastised Beatrice for telling him nothing of what she was doing: 'you can hardly have lost all the interest that I believe you formerly had in many things as to which we have written. One day you will no doubt tell me all about it, face to face: meanwhile I shall assume that you are really a friend and sincerely interested in your friends.'

Beatrice replied by return sending him two chapters of her book of Co-operation.

I should have written to you more fully but I partly thought that the correspondence had dropped on your side. I am always interested to hear any news you may have about subjects in which we are both of us interested, though I have very little to tell in return.

I am working on steadily at my book ... I should enjoy the writing of it very much if I did not feel pressed for time and space, and if I was not oppressed with my own audacity in attempting to re-found the Co-operative Movement in a 2/– book of 220 pages....

We are having lovely weather here: and if I were not so oppressed with the burden of the little book I should be enjoying it....

Yours very sincerely
Beatrice Potter.

At the beginning of March Sidney replied, still doing his best not to tread beyond the bounds of formal friendship. He told her that he liked the chapters she had sent him of her book. 'I have little to criticise,' he told her. 'I have marked one or two places where your meaning is obscure.' He went on to tell her something of his activities and his plans. His book on the Eight Hours movement was finished and he advised Beatrice to take on a collaborator for the book on Trade Unionism which she was hoping to write, despite the fact that he had not found his own partner 'perfectly satisfactory. He is not energetic enough to be yoke fellow with me!' He wrote in a stilted way but he could not finish the letter without unbending.

You say you have had fine weather: we have had a week's continuous fog. I thought more than once of the garden at Box – and of a certain rose now withered.

This is not the letter I meant to write, but there is no use in you and me quarrelling. We can never be quite ordinary acquaintances to each other. Our friendship has been consecrated by a great

117

sorrow. I have suffered a good deal these three months – already three months! – and I know you would have given a good deal not to have made me suffer. . . .

I have no right to *extort* a friendship out of you. But if you feel impelled to be a real friend, be absolutely frank and candid with me. . . . Do not refuse to see me when you are in London: you have told me nothing about that. Is all this asking too much? Nay, if it is asking anything that you would not spontaneously desire to concede, it is impossible.

Sidney Webb.

Beatrice's book was now almost finished and she too was thinking about the next step in her career. She was keen to go ahead with her idea of a history of Trade Unions, which would be a natural sequel to her study of the Co-operatives. Both subjects had been neglected by professional historians and though she was an amateur she was now regarded as something of an authority on such social questions. 'Ghastly report that I am to be appointed a member of the Royal Commission on the Capital and Labour questions,' she noted on 7 March, though she secretly hankered after an appointment of this kind as a recognition of her capacities and interests. She had also been asked to deliver a series of lectures on the Co-operative movement at University Hall in the middle of April. With all these demands on her she felt overwrought – 'I feel as I should like to throw down my work and cry,' she wrote in her diary. 'But it is all miserable weakness. Oh how detestable public life is to a woman! And yet a sort of fate drags one into it.' In a letter to Sidney she conveyed some of her self-doubts and sense of loneliness, and his reply had a flat, dispirited air as he told her frankly what he thought of her book.

It would not be honest if I did not own to a disappointment. . . . I think perhaps that I expected too much from your literary art. . . . I honestly believe that what I have seen in proof will read very effectively. You have taken care to send me no more proofs.

Shall I be quite candid? Do not take it amiss if I confess to a slight feeling that you have taken too long over it. The book will not be a *very* great work....

Do not suppose, because I 'run on' in this way that I am not lonely too. It is possible to be as lonely in London as elsewhere. I am conscious of a longing for letters and friends; but also of a horrible shrinking from both.... The great secret of life is not to expect too much from it. After all, the world is neither black nor white, but grey ... and only children cry for sugar instead. (I am a child.)

Yours
Sidney Webb.

Such comments about her work made Beatrice herself doubtful. She had taken seven months to write a book of little more than two hundred pages. 'What is it?' she asked herself; 'a clever political pamphlet or a sound contribution? My former self doubts my present self: which I wonder will prove the wisest – the cold blooded investigator or the would-be reformer: intellect or heart?' Despite his critical comments Beatrice sent Sidney a friendly reply.

Dear Mr Webb.

Pray do not think that I should be better pleased with a favourable opinion.... Even in work done – I should always value your outspoken opinion: I give it full weight even if I do not altogether agree with it.

I do not believe that the new life you are plunging into will injure you; I believe that you have *that* in you that will be proof both against the failure or friction of public life and also against the inflation of actual or seeming power. Failure and success will probably come to you – flattery and mortification – but I have faith that your self-devotion is tempered with self-humility....

Certainly we will see each other in London. I will send you presently the remainder of my proofs....

I feel horribly nervous about my lectures but am trying to console myself with the arguments that it will be 'good enough' not to be a disgrace....

Ever yours
Beatrice Potter.

Both Beatrice and Sidney were expressing their nervousness in facing the world as they took on greater responsibilities. Sidney had now decided 'to make the plunge' and give up his Civil Service career, even though he had the feeling that the task was too great, 'amid dangers for which I had not sufficient weapons, in money, in strength or in friends'. In these circumstances Sidney was keenly aware that his need for Beatrice was greater than ever, and he wrote to her with earnest frankness on 6 April.

Still, it may come out all right after all – especially if I am not left to bear all the weight alone. Do not be afraid that I am going to revert to the forbidden topic. I will never ask you to make a sacrifice for me.... But you can help me – very likely save me – by your influence if you like.

I think, perhaps, that you have some little responsibility for using that influence.... Let me see you frequently: let me tell you all my difficulties; and help me....

You probably do not realise how I am living. I do not number my hours of work, because I do nothing else. I see no friends, save in the work. I have not read a book for months. I have not been to a theatre or concert or picture gallery in London for years.... It is a cramped and joyless life, but I see no chance of changing it. I feel like the London cabhorse who could not be taken out of the shafts lest he should fall down! I tell you this that you may see what your friendship has already been to me: and what it might be in the future....

All this will sound very egotistical and repining. I am afraid this past week has been a bad one for me. The East wind depressed my animal spirits, and I have piles of work to do....

Are we not, *in all essentials*, back to where we were nine months ago? Honestly and frankly, I acquiesce in your decision. My feelings are unchanged but I see your point of view. I am prepared to serve your life, and to ask nothing whatever in return, save only your work for Socialism, and such share of friendship as you choose to give. You have put it upon me to show you that I can be unselfish, and I don't think you will have any cause to be disappointed.

Yours in perfect sincerity
Sidney Webb.

It was a touching letter and Beatrice could not but be affected by it. She had come to London to deliver her lectures on Co-operation and many of her friends and relatives were there to hear her debut as a public lecturer. The success did not mitigate the strain: 'Oh! the nervous irritability of the next day.' *The Times* had asked for an advance summary of what she was to say, and Beatrice did not feel equal to this additional task. Alice Green, with whom she was staying, suggested that Sidney could do what was wanted – perhaps seeing an opportunity of helping the estranged pair over the embarrassment of meeting each other. And so Beatrice turned to Sidney for help, just as she had done on their first meeting over a year before. Sidney responded at once and together they drew up the report for *The Times*.

They were back on easy terms and in May, with Mrs Green for company, they travelled down to Lincoln for the Co-operative Congress. The year before, at Glasgow, they had made their 'working compact'; now on their return from Lincoln, Beatrice at last gave way. Sidney's persistent devotion had finally touched her heart, and her own need triumphed over her fear and her pride. 'I cannot tell how things will settle themselves,' she wrote in her diary afterwards. 'I think probably in his way.'

Sidney recalled a year later the telling moment when Beatrice did not withdraw her hand from his. And Beatrice, too, remembered 'that evening at Devonshire House – in the twilight when we for the first time embraced – how well I remember the happiness tempered by great anxiety'.

In her diary Beatrice tried to put into words what had led her to change her mind: 'His resolute patient affection, his honest care for my welfare – helping and correcting me – a growing distrust of a self-absorbed life and the egotism of successful work – all these feelings are making for our eventual union – the joining together of our resources – mental and material – to serve together the "commonwealth". But if I marry,' she went on, 'though I shall be drawn to it by affection and gratitude, it will be an act of renunciation of self and not of indulgence of self, as it would have been in the other case. Perhaps, therefore it will be blessed for both of us.'

Sidney was bewildered and overawed by this dramatic reversal of his fortunes. 'I am still a little in a dream,' he wrote to Beatrice next day.' 'I have not yet fully realised all your kindness. But at any rate it is a brilliant rose-coloured morning and I pitied the man on the omnibus who said the rain was very cold. For me there was no rain and no cold.'

There were still practical problems to be settled. They agreed that while Richard Potter still lived they could make no definite plans and that their engagement must be kept a secret even from family and close friends. Beatrice realized that her father would have been deeply pained by the idea that she should marry a physically unattractive socialist without means, and she was determined to spare him that shock in the last phase of his life. In fact Sidney was more confident about his ability to support a decent professional standard of living. 'I cannot imagine that we could rightfully spend as much as we are likely jointly to have. Everyone tells me that I can earn £1,000 or even £2,000 a year if I choose,' he told Beatrice; 'do you not suppose that I would not work myself to the bone before I would allow you to miss any one comfort necessary for your fullest efficiency?' He was confident and optimistic. 'Do not be afraid of the future,' he told Beatrice; 'meanwhile let us get all we can out of the present.' They planned to take a holiday in June. 'I don't care to look forward even to June!' wrote Sidney. 'I cannot exhaust the present moment, which is *délire, extase, ivresse*, because I am writing to you.'

Relaxing in the beautiful Norwegian scenery with Sidney, Graham Wallas and a bright young Fabienne called Clara Brigden, Beatrice thought over the new life that was beginning for her. Even now there were moments when she disconsolately wondered 'whether from my point of view I have been wise'. Her diary shows that she was only too well aware that it was a curious match.

The world will wonder. On the face of it, it seems an extraordinary end to the once brilliant Beatrice Potter, to marry an ugly little man with no social position and less means – whose only recommendation – so some may say – is a certain pushing ability. And I am not 'in love', not as I was. But I see something else in him – a fine intellect, and a warm-heartedness, a power of self-subordination and self devotion for the 'common good'.... His feeling is the passionate love of an emotional man, mine the growing tenderness of the mother touched with the dependence of the woman on the help of a strong lover.... He is in a state of happy exaltation – I am beginning to feel at rest and assured.

As they wandered over the Norwegian moorland, hand in hand, they discussed their future. Beatrice encouraged Sidney to seek election to the London County Council. 'We are both of us second-rate minds,' she presciently observed, 'but we are curiously combined – I am the investigator, and he the executor and we have a wide and varied experience of men and things between us. We have also an unearned salary. This forms our unique circumstances.' Beatrice was determined not to become absorbed in the details of domestic life and she planned, with Sidney's help, to press on with her trade-union book. 'For we have a great responsibility laid upon us,' she wrote. 'Not only has each one of us faculty and the opportunity of using it, but both together – the two united form a true marriage of fellow-workers – a perfect fellowship: it is for us to show that such a marriage may be durable and persisting.'

Beatrice's loyalty was very quickly tested, for on 14 July, after her return from Norway, she went to have tea with Mary Booth, one of the few people to whom she had confided her secret. Although she had counted on her cousin for support, it was clear at once that the Booths did not much care for the idea of her marriage to Sidney. She was also hurt that the Booths made no mention of her book despite the fact that she had given them a copy before her holiday: 'it was not unnatural that I should sit down and cry – not about their not thinking much of my little book – but of their not really caring to know him'.

Mary Booth was not so unsympathetic as Beatrice believed, for the next day she wrote to her husband to tell him that Beatrice 'looks remarkably well, young, pretty and blooming, like her old self. Norway has set her up. She is evidently happy and believes in Mr Sidney Webb thoroughly.... Heroics over the self-sacrifice of living on an income of about £1500 sound quaintly in my ears; but all the same I think better of the affair after seeing Beatrice.' And at the same time she sent Beatrice a friendly letter. 'It would be of no use to pretend that we are not sorry it is so,' she admitted; 'we will prepare ourselves to think and expect all the good we wish for you in the life you have chosen.' Charles Booth also wrote kindly to Beatrice: 'It will give me great pleasure to become better acquainted with Mr Webb and I feel I shall gain much from a close and cousinly contact with the school of thought and action of which he is so brilliant a representative.' These polite words were not sufficient. Beatrice had hoped for more, and she sadly concluded that the engagement had cast a shadow over her old intimacy with the Booths. But there was nothing she could do. 'If they cease to feel warmly to me – well – I must think of them tenderly and go on my way.'

She now spent as much time as she could in London to be with Sidney. Beatrice had considered other able young men as assistants for her proposed study of trade-union history, but once matters had been settled with Sidney, his collaboration on the book was taken for granted. The prospects of such a partnership had been a vital factor in Sidney's campaign to win her as a comrade, a colleague and a wife. They met every day at 64 Avenue Road, Herbert Spencer's house in St John's Wood, while its owner was away for the summer. There, with what Beatrice coyly described as 'breaks for human nature', they began the research for their first joint work: 'then lunch, cigarettes, a little more "human nature" and then another two hours work. A cup of tea, walk to the Athenaeum, work at the Social Science records in the library and dinner.'

Sidney had returned from Norway full of joy and hope. 'I am as brown as a Chilian, and probably pounds heavier through the wonderful holiday we have had,' he wrote to Beatrice; 'surely no one was ever quite so fortunate before . . . Goodbye, dearest, *dearest* Beatrice. Teach me *how* I may show my love for you.' But he returned to London to find his father, who suffered from bronchitis, and a weak heart, had become a chronic invalid, and on 21 July he died suddenly. 'Dearest,' Sidney wrote Beatrice, 'this "jars" a little on our happiness, but it is better so. . . . I am not in any way *overwhelmed* with grief; and it seems much more important to me to care for those who are left. But still I think "Poor Father". He led an upright, modest, humble life. . . .'

Beatrice had her own domestic responsibilities back at Box. She said nothing about her future intentions either to Mary Playne or to Kate Courtney, who was on a visit to Longfords, and she took a sardonic and teasing pleasure in keeping them in the dark.

This morning I had a walk with Kate. She was very friendly, and in the course of the talk exclaimed 'I wonder whether you will marry'. I sedately replied that I thought it highly probable – but that in any case marriage with me would be subordinate to work. . . . She asked me whether I liked 'Sidney Webb as much after the tour as before'. I answered enigmatically 'I like both those men immensely', and then told her that Graham Wallas was coming to spend a week on the 26th. . . . This morning I began 6.30 and read Brentano's Guilds in the hour before lunch. . . . Then lunch, a cigarette, a sleep, cup of tea, more arranging – $1\frac{1}{2}$ [hours] reading to Father. And then I suddenly bethought me there *might* be a letter at the Post Office. So I popped on an old skirt and a mackintosh and trudged through the rain to Minchinhampton and found what I desired. No, dear, I do not even look at your photograph. It is too hideous, for anything. Do be done in a gray suit by Elliot and Fry and let me have your *head only* – it is the head only that I am marrying! . . . I send you the bunch of wild hyacinths I picked that spring day in the Longford woods, just near to the bank we sat on 18 months ago. They have dried up – while our love has grown. Now, dearest, goodnight; Let us both try to be faithful stewards. Let me learn from you.

Always your loving comrade

Beatrice Potter.

Beatrice was determined that her engagement should help rather than hinder her work and she threw herself vigorously into research. When she was in London she went down to the Home Office to read Blue Books. 'There I sit in that big official apartment strewn with despatch boxes in solitary glory with the roar of Whitehall below.' She met Sidney wherever and whenever she could, even if it were at a railway junction where their routes crossed when she was bound for a trade-union gathering and he was on his way to a speaking engagement. At the beginning of September, for instance, she went to Newcastle to attend the Trades Union Congress but she stopped off at Birmingham for a brief meeting with Sidney. 'Certainly we are daring in our unconventionality,' she wrote in her diary as these meetings became more frequent, 'mostly meeting at a hotel and spending 24 hours there.'

It was the beginning of September when Sidney finally resigned from the Colonial Office. 'Dearest, but for you,' he wrote to Beatrice, 'I should today be trembling, wondering whether I had done right. I don't think you quite realise how much you have saved me from, in the way of worry, anxiety and fear.' After the Trades Union Congress Beatrice stayed in the North-East to continue her research – drudging in office archives and trudging from interview to interview. She missed Sidney but they kept up a busy correspondence. 'Now, goodbye dearest one,' she wrote after a week away.

126

'We need not love each other the less because with both of us our work stands first and our union second. We can give each other security in the widest sense – so long as we can face the separation which will be essential to free and full pursuit of our work.'

'Dearest I do miss you,' Sidney wrote on 14 September, thinking that he would not see her for another two weeks. 'I don't in the least object. I would infinitely rather endure to lose you for a year rather than have you neglect your work for my sake – you know, and believe, I am sure, that this is the exact truth. We could not love each other so well, loved we not our work and duty more.'

There were moments when Beatrice despaired at the magnitude of the task she had undertaken and in such moments of depression felt her old doubts about marriage. 'Do you know, dearest,' she wrote, 'I must confess that at times I have regretted that my days of free and unnoticed investigation were numbered.' She did not see how she could make a good wife and at the same time make a really good book. 'Every now and then I feel I have got into a hole out of which I can't struggle. I love you – but I love my work better!'

'Dearest,' Sidney replied,

I must not hide from you that your letter came on me rather as a constriction of the heart. I am grieved to think that your loss by your love stands out so to you in this mood. Dearest, if you really think I am going to be a drag on you I shall be very very grieved. But I am *not*. . . . My dearest love, don't be despondent. . . . Be happy, dearest, and have patience. I am worn out with work, but I can and will spare time to give you a hand. You have made a splendid beginning; and all is well.

Early in October Sidney was free from the Colonial Office and he joined Beatrice in Newcastle. 'With our usual caution,' she explained, 'I have taken a private sitting-room (he staying at another hotel) and he spends the day with me in the capacity of "private secretary".' It was a 'blessed' time and Beatrice soon recovered her spirits. Sidney took over all the accumulated work – 'and while I have been lying on the sofa he has been busily abstracting and extracting, amply rewarded he says by a few brief intervals of "human nature" over the cigarettes or the afternoon cup of tea.' She admitted that 'without his help I doubt whether I could have got through the work – I have too little staying power for the extent of my brain'.

When Sidney returned to London after their 'blessed fortnight' together Beatrice remained to continue her inquiries at Durham. Suddenly one day she discovered that she was travelling on the same train as Chamberlain and his wife, who were on the way to a big political rally at Sunderland. The encounter caused her no pangs. 'I shuddered as I imagined the life I had missed. Now, indeed, I can bless him for his clear understanding of my deficiencies for the great role of "walking gentlewoman" to the play of *Chamberlain*.' Sidney's visit had in fact reassured her as to the decision she had made. 'Now dear boy,' she wrote to Sidney, 'finding we had a very happy fortnight together – I feel much more confident that our marriage will not interfere with our own work. Get a new tie and string to your pince-nez and look after your pronunciation. You can't afford not to be careful about externals you can improve! You have been very sweet and kind to me all the time. That book *must* be a success.'

Beatrice returned to Box at the beginning of November to find her father in a miserable state. 'I cannot believe that he can last long,' she wrote to Sidney, and she found it 'sad to see the brave old man linger on in this wretched state of discomfort and weariness.' She still kept her engagement a secret from her sisters; indeed her unconventional life and her advanced political views had further estranged her from them. 'You know we are absolutely ignorant of Beatrice's life,' Theresa commented to Miss Darling, the companion, 'she might be a *man* and we should be no more ignorant – she never consults us or confides in us.' Beatrice was grateful to her sisters for the freedom they had given her from her domestic ties but she feared that any confidences about her work and private life might make them embarrassed and critical of her. She still grieved at the estrangement from the Booths and she was beginning to find the continuing secret a strain: 'after Xmas, when we again begin working together,' she wrote to Sidney in November, 'I will write and tell my sisters. Then we can begin the New Year openly and face everything openly and together.'

Sidney, for all his happiness and optimism, was not insensitive to the difficulties that lay ahead. He knew that Beatrice's friends and relatives would find him unattractive and unsympathetic but he was philosophic about it. 'I am sure I shall be capable of *wishing* you to keep up your own friends even if they are not mine. Of course I would rather be liked than disliked,' he wrote, 'but I think we ought to recognise how that is often impossible. I can't help it being "Beauty and the Beast" – if only it is not a case of Titania and Bottom!'

The winter days passed peacefully; cold mists swept over the hills and the wind howled about the house as Richard Potter lingered on. Beatrice took rides and walked through the lanes; she read; she arranged the material she had gathered for her book; Wallas came down for a visit and Ella Pycroft was another guest and they both stayed on over Christmas. 'This will be the last Xmas Day that we need be apart,' Beatrice wrote to Sidney on Christmas Day; 'today I feel happy but serious about the future. Dear one, I will try to repay your love and devotion and to make our home and happiness together – in spite of your "professional" wife.' As the year ended Beatrice looked back on it in her diary. 'The year has been uneventful,' she wrote. 'My engagement was a very deliberate step each condition thought out thoroughly; now it is an unconscious happiness.'

'It has been a good year to us, dearest,' wrote Sidney – 'a heavenly year to me though it opened gloomily enough. But it is *the* year of my life – there can be no other like it.'

CHAPTER TEN

Exit Beatrice Potter

RICHARD POTTER died on the morning of New Year's Day 1892. 'Few men have attracted and given more devoted affection,' wrote Beatrice, and she told Sidney that 'we will try to live our lives with dignity and devotion as Father did according to his lights in his day.' It was a stressful and touching time for her. 'I feel rather weak and cold,' she wrote, 'a little bit anxious about the future – because I don't feel strong and able. But I dare say I shall get into harness again.' She felt the weight of death in the house and the large assembly of sisters and brothers-in-law asking questions about her future. Maggie begged her not to cut herself adrift from the family and to marry within her own 'class'; such remarks only made her feel more weighed down by the declaration she was about to make to them. Sidney wrote to her each day with letters of support and love: 'Dearest, this is the beginning of a new year for both of us,' he wrote when he heard the news, 'and you, for the first time, are *quite* free to give yourself to your work and to me. I will do all I can to make you gain thereby.... Sweet! that I love you better than ever is perhaps not much guarantee: but over your father's death let us cement our agreement again that all we do shall be for "Social Service" as far as we know how.'

Beatrice had decided to break the news to her sisters after the funeral, but a report of the engagement leaked into the press and rumours began to fly about. Sidney, to make sure the secret was kept, even sent his telegrams in German, and did his best to stop the news spreading until Beatrice told her sisters. She was so nervously conscious of their disapproval that she wrote somewhat defensively to explain to them how things stood. 'The whole of this week I have been feeling rather miserable because I have wished to tell you of my engagement to Mr Sidney Webb, but I have not had the courage to do so,' she wrote to Mary Playne;

And now dear sister you must do what you feel inclined. If your dislike to Sidney Webb is so firmly rooted (after once seeing him!) that you cannot hold yourself to speak of him as your future brother-in-law it would be better that we should not discuss it, in which case it might be better for us not to meet.... But I need not say that should my marriage mean a break in the old tie between us I shall be genuinely and permanently grieved.

To Lallie, as the eldest sister, Beatrice sent a full and frank explanation with details of Sidney's career and background. 'And now let me say quite frankly that I am sincerely grieved that my marriage is not one which will give my sisters, in the first instance, much satisfaction,' she went on defensively. 'Superficially your new brother-in-law will have little to recommend him. He is very small and ugly! he has none of the *savoir-faire* which comes from a leisurely up-bringing and of course he has none of the social position which springs from great possession and family connections.' But she expressed her confidence that her sisters would not let any superficial deficiencies stand in the way of an appreciation of Sidney's good qualities – 'of warm and generous sympathy and quick perception'.

As Beatrice had hoped, the family generally behaved with benevolence and good sense. Even Mary, for all her prejudices, was generous. 'Personally I shall begin my acquaintance with him as though I had never seen him with a desire to like him because he is the man who has been able to win

your heart and whom you believe will make you happy.'
Georgina, too, did her best to allay Beatrice's suspicions:
'You say we are prejudiced against Mr Webb, but as I have
only seen him for half an hour that can hardly be a strong
feeling on my part,' she wrote. 'We may not be quite kindred
spirits to each other but if he makes you happy we shall certainly appreciate him in the end.' When Kate heard the news
she was surprised and admitted that it was not altogether welcome. 'But the more I think of it, the more I feel certain that
he must have some very fine qualities to have won your affection,' she wrote to Beatrice. 'We shall be very keen now to
meet him.'

Even the brothers-in-law wrote kindly. 'It is the kind of
marriage I always expected you would make,' wrote Alfred
Cripps. 'Difference of opinion is a small matter where it
is genuine and tolerant.' And Henry Hobhouse thought Sidney was to be congratulated 'on having (among his many
successes in life) secured for his wife the last and (to put it
very mildly) not the least of the great sisterhood'.

It was not long before Beatrice brought Sidney to dinner
at the Courtneys, and Alfred and Theresa Cripps were there
to meet him. Kate, who had not met him before and had
heard only unflattering accounts, was favourably impressed.
'He was quiet, perhaps shy,' she noted in her diary, 'but he
looks strong and able though not much of a figure of a man,
and I hope we may like him. Beatrice seems quietly happy
and confident of the future, and she has a softness of expression and manner which looks as if her feelings were engaged.'
Two days later Alfred and Theresa in turn entertained Sidney
and Beatrice to meet other members of the family – Lallie,
Blanche and Willie Cripps and Daniel Meinertzhagen. Kate
was also a guest on this occasion and after this second meeting
she noted: 'Yes, I *think* we may like this new brother-in-law
whom we certainly should not have chosen.'

Sidney, too, was making his assessment of his new relatives. 'Dearest, my impression is that your sisters are not very

able women in the intellectual way. Really, Mrs Holt is the cleverest of the lot: and your trained intellect positively stands out as quite alien to them all. . . . I don't wonder that you got on best with the said husbands. It must have been difficult to have any really intellectual conversation with the wives. And the husbands are a set of remarkably able men each in his own way.' For all that he was not ungenerous. 'But I don't want to "run down" your sisters. They have all been exceedingly kind, and they are at least as clever as the ordinary woman of society, and the ordinary mother of a family. Only, you see, one expected *your* sisters to be something more.'

Beatrice agreed with him. 'You are quite right,' she wrote; 'my sisters are not intellectual women. They are shrewd women of the world with good motherly hearts and their fair share of mother wit – but they have never gone in for training their minds. Lallie, Theresa and Margaret have the most natural intellect – more than I had to begin with.' The more often Sidney met his new relatives the more he realized that he and Beatrice would see little of them after their marriage.

Sidney, for his part, had to introduce Beatrice to his family, who were now living at Park Village East in a modest but pretty house near Regent's Park: 'the little home away in a small street,' wrote Beatrice: 'the little mother – frail and shaking with palsy – the energetic warmhearted plain body of a sister, a stalwart German woman who acted as general servant – have become a new surrounding to my life – a new scene laid in the lower middle class'. She soon adjusted to these unfamiliar surroundings. 'The dingy and crowded little work room with gas fire where Sidney and I sit the evening through, happy and unconscious in our love for the other. And gradually the feeling of unwished for dislike to ugly and small surroundings disappeared in the blessedness of love.'

Nevertheless, Beatrice was very conscious that her old life was now over and that she was marrying beneath her. It was true that by her family's prosperous standards she and Sidney would have to live very modestly. Yet they would have more than enough for the way they proposed to live. Once her father's estate was settled Beatrice's legacy of £26,000 would give her an income of about £1,000 a year and with this security to underpin Sidney's journalistic earnings there would be enough to enable Sidney to think of a political career. He had already taken the first step in December when he was selected as the Progressive candidate for Deptford in the forthcoming County Council Elections. The Progressives, who had won a majority on the newly formed Council which ruled the capital, were the London spokesmen for the advanced Liberals, and the Fabians found them congenial allies in their campaign for municipal reform. Sidney now spent much of his time in south-east London preparing for the election at the beginning of March and Beatrice went up to Manchester to continue her trade-union research. 'I wish I had you here to relieve the loneliness of the off times, and to visit you after your Deptford election. I think I could come up on the Wednesday or Thursday of *the* week – I shan't expect you to be anything but fractious. I will soothe and comfort you – and if you are defeated I will spend Sunday kissing you! Ever your devoted comrade, Beatrice Potter.'

Sidney, however, was not defeated. He proved to be a talented election organizer and he won an impressive victory, polling unexpectedly well and securing twice as many votes as his opponent. 'The result was not declared until after 1 a.m.', Sidney wrote to Wallas next day on 6 March, 'I made a little speech etc and then was lifted shoulder high by an excited mob, carried downstairs to the imminent risk of scraping the ceiling with my nose, and so out into the road amid a fearful uproar.' Beatrice, unfortunately, was not there to cheer. She had been struck down with influenza and spent two weeks in bed. Sidney rushed up to Manchester to see her as soon as the election was over, and they went on together to Liverpool to stay with Lallie and her husband.

'It was nice of the Holts to speak pleasantly of me,' Sidney told Beatrice afterwards, 'and as regards the pronunciation it must come sweetly to the ear of the teacher to hear the scholar praised. They are very nice people.'

The visit was one more in the round of invitations from Beatrice's sisters. 'I am a little afraid of these sisters,' Sidney told Beatrice, 'with all their kindness and smothering me with invitations. But it is of course only natural that they should "want to know".' The Courtneys, active Liberals themselves, now asked him regularly to dinner; he went for tea to Theresa Cripps, and at the Hobhouses he met Lord Hobhouse who was an important Liberal figure on the LCC. 'This LCC election has gone far to redeem our marriage in the eyes of your family,' he wrote to Beatrice. 'They don't fear for their own incomes, and they think I am more of a personage than they supposed.' All the same, this run of hospitality was something of a strain for Sidney. 'I have missed you a lot,' he wrote to Beatrice at the end of March before going to yet another family dinner. 'And I am a little afraid of the Meinertzhagens tonight – afraid I mean of seeming to them more than necessarily mean and small and ugly, with my bad cold.' The evening, however, passed agreeably. 'I think they will simply wonder what you can see in that commonplace ugly little man.'

It was a time of reconciliation. Even the Booths were friendly again and Mary Booth was affectionate to Beatrice – 'like her old self'. The only family friend who would not accept the match was Herbert Spencer. 'I cannot congratulate you,' he told Beatrice bluntly, 'that would be insincere.' Beatrice did her best to get him to see it differently; she told the old man that her family had taken it benevolently and that Mr Webb himself was a 'man of capacity and determination' with a 'sweet temper' and 'an excellent brother and son'. But it soon became clear to Beatrice that Spencer's objection was not personal but a matter of principle. He no longer wished Beatrice to be his literary executor; 'It would not do for my reputation that I should be openly connected with an avowed and prominent socialist,' he told her. All the same the eminent philosopher realized that anyone who set out to write his biography would need to call on Beatrice's literary skill and her personal knowledge of him. The difficulty was resolved when, from a sense of duty, Beatrice offered to help but without acknowledgement. Spencer agreed, 'satisfied about his reputation and I at ease with the dictates of filial piety'. Beatrice wondered whether it was in effect the close of their long friendship. 'Poor old man!' she mused, 'the shell of a great spirit slowly dwindled down from a consuming egotism and vanity.'

The spring months of separation were difficult for Beatrice and Sidney but they were determined to stay with their separate tasks until their marriage which was now arranged to take place on 26 July. 'Dearest, these four months are going to be a bit of a trial,' Sidney wrote on 25 March. 'I am so sorry not to be able to be with you, but it is our own deliberate choice and I think we were right though I hate it now – I miss you so much.' It was Sidney who made the practical arrangements. He reported to Beatrice that after eighteen days' residence of one or other of the parties and at a cost of £2 9s. od. for the licence they could be married at the St Pancras Vestry Hall – 'an ordinary "official" looking place,' he wrote, 'and the Registrar's office is of ordinary office type, neither better nor worse. I fear the Courtneys will think it "mean", but you won't mind, dearest?'

At Easter-time Beatrice came south for two weeks' holiday. She and Sidney spent four days in a Sussex village near Arundel with Graham Wallas and 'the light-hearted Bernard Shaw'. Each meeting now with Sidney only confirmed her happiness and she felt lonely without him. 'Never did I imagine such happiness,' she wrote in her diary. 'May I deserve it.' Back in Liverpool and Manchester there was work to be done and Beatrice then visited other towns in the north – Wigan and Macclesfield. She now had a secretary,

Frank Galton, one of the students in a course Sidney had been
giving at the Workingmen's College, and although Beatrice's sisters didn't quite approve, suggesting some impro-
priety, Galton joined Beatrice in Lancashire to help with the
research. It was a busy time. 'Galton called at 9 and we went
together to the office,' Beatrice told Sidney, 'there I worked
till 12.30, went out to do some shopping, had lunch – interviewed the secretary of the Employers' Building Federation,
worked over their minutes of 1877–8,' she went on, 'dictated
the miners' minutes to Galton until 5.30, had some tea, and
took the train up to Durham, interviewed Ashton of the
Miners, bagged a huge parcel of minute books and dragged
them back here. And now I am supping off cold meat and
ginger ale and writing to you between whiles.'

Sidney, meanwhile, was devoting most of his energies to
the LCC. He had already been appointed chairman of one of
its committees. 'I shall be pretty full up for a month or two
and cannot hope to help you just at present. Be Patient!' he
told Beatrice. He was also caught up in the political excitement of the General Election which was to take place that summer. A group of Radicals were pressing for his nomination
for a parliamentary seat at Gateshead, but he assured Beatrice
that 'I have no intention of becoming candidate *anywhere*
for the General Election this time'. He was more disposed
to work behind the scenes within the Fabian Society, now
at the peak of its reputation and influence. They were
recruiting new members everywhere, organizing lectures up
and down the country, issuing pamphlets and providing
Liberal candidates with a radical programme of reform. 'We
are sending out *thousands* of Fabian tracts every day – there
is a daily growing demand from paying sources,' he told Beatrice. 'I think we are doing a good bit of political education
over this election.'

Sidney, as usual, was in the thick of the fight and he gave
what time he could to electioneering. He spoke for his friend
Costelloe and a candidate at Woolwich. He was enjoying

himself. Separation from Beatrice was the only flaw: 'Dearest I *am* happy, but it is terrible to be away from you,' and he worried about her. 'I am horribly afraid you are overworking yourself. It is hard that we cannot be together but don't make it harder for me by making me anxious about you. Is this part of the "husband's manner" that you already notice in me? Dear, I *do* feel responsible for you – and if you don't mind I shall be coming down to prevent you getting ill,' he told her. 'We have brilliant weather, even warm, but there is an East wind and I have a little cold and cough – just enough to make me think I should like to be with you to be petted. I could pet back!'

If Sidney was developing a 'husband's manner', Beatrice was developing a wifely one. Sidney went north to visit her at the beginning of June: 'How delightful it will be to be together again,' she told him. 'I have been meaning to advise you *not* to bring that thick flannel nightshirt. I notice you always have a cold when you return home and I am pretty sure that it comes from changing from flannel to cotton nightshirts. It is far more dangerous than the bare chance of damp sheets – an article which I, in all my wanderings, have never met with. And in this weather you would find the flannel insupportable.'

They spent a happy few days together. 'My own dear darling,' Beatrice wrote afterwards. 'I felt a lump in my throat as I saw you drive away – the little lodging with the rain dripping down onto the pavement outside seemed so dreary – and I felt lonesome.' But she was soon at work – there were interviews with a factory inspector and an alderman, minutes to read, and then a visit to Preston. 'If only I keep fit for work,' she wrote, 'and we live well within our income!' Beatrice, with no experience of living on a limited budget, was now trying to reassure herself that there would be enough money for all they planned to do. Although she did not want Sidney to go into Parliament – 'that enemy of domesticity' – for four years or so, it was a long-term plan that he would do so, and money would have to be put aside for that. She told Sidney that she was now living at the rate of £448 a year. She added:

I hope you will help me to be economical – your tendency will be to press me to have everything I want. It will not do to stint the work – and here of course is the difficulty – one's personal expenditure is so mixed up with indirect working expenses; but we must not get lax.... We ought not only to be able to do our work and put on one side £200 a year for Parliamentary expenses but I should like to have something at the end of each year to give one of our poorer fellow-workers.'

As their wedding-day approached they found their separation an increasing strain. 'I do miss you,' Beatrice wrote. 'I am glad that we shall soon be married – it does not seem natural to be apart now.'

'Dear I do love you so,' wrote Sidney, 'that I am not sure that I am unconsciously constructing a new theory of the universe,' he went on, 'in which you are the centre of things. Really it is high time we were married lest I get quite absurd.'

At the end of June, Beatrice ordered her wedding dress, at a cost of £4, in a light grey material. 'I am sure you will look sweet in your new dress,' Sidney told her '– even if dark blue silk does suit you better – because you are (I am *so* thankful for this) happy in what you are undertaking. We will go and choose the prettiest little brooch we can find. I am glad you will let me give you this little token. You have so few gifts from me – save that everything I do is now done for you.'

As the day drew near Sidney told Beatrice that his mother was chuckling one evening over dinner at some joke; she 'at last let it out, viz, that this was the last Sunday I had to do what I liked in!' Sidney took such chaffs in good part. Everyone, indeed, was in cheerful mood for all the private reservations and criticisms in confidence.

The wedding took place at 11.45 a.m. on 23 July at St Pancras Vestry. It was a simple ceremony. Indeed, as Sidney had predicted, Kate Courtney thought it 'a prosaic, almost sordid ceremony – our civil marriages are not conducted with much dignity and seem rather to suggest a certain shadiness in the contracting parties. But Bee looked good – serious and hand-some.' Apart from Graham Wallas, who was the best man, the rest of the wedding party were all members of the family – Sidney's sister, brother and sister-in-law, the Courtneys, Alfred Cripps, Blanche Cripps and Maggie Hobhouse, the Dyson Williams and the Booths. There was a wedding breakfast afterwards given by the Holts, as the senior members of the family, at the Euston Railway Hotel. 'I shrink from the wedding feast,' Sidney had told Beatrice beforehand, but Kate declared that it 'went off very well'.

'The only thing I regret is parting with my *name* – I *do* resent that,' Beatrice told Sidney, and she wrote in her diary on her wedding-day: 'Exit Beatrice Potter, Enter Beatrice Webb or rather (Mrs) Sidney Webb for I lose alas! both names.'

Epilogue

THE marriage of Beatrice and Sidney Webb was happy and rewarding, and it lasted for half a century. They followed the course they had set when they made their working compact in Glasgow in 1890. Sidney became a leading member of the London County Council and a notable educational reformer. He did not go into the House of Commons until 1922 and although Beatrice thought he would enjoy being an MP Sidney found it less agreeable than he had hoped. Nevertheless, when the first Labour Government was formed in 1924 he became a member of the Cabinet as President of the Board of Trade. When the Labour Party again came to power in 1929 Sidney was appointed Secretary of State for the Colonies, the same government department in which he had made his career as a civil servant, and by a strange quirk of fate both his Cabinet offices had been held by Joseph Chamberlain fifty years before.

While Beatrice was less of a public figure she also played a part in public life, most notably as a member of the Royal Commission on the Poor Law which was set up in 1906. With Sidney's help, she had written the famous Minority Report of that Commission which laid the foundation for much of the welfare state in Britain. When Sidney went into Parliament Beatrice had more time to herself and she decided to write her autobiography. It appeared in two volumes – *My Apprenticeship* and *Our Partnership* – and was made up for the most part from the revealing diaries which she kept all her life.

The Webbs were also energetic collaborators. In 1895 they founded the London School of Economics. In 1913 they launched the weekly magazine, the *New Statesman*. They wrote a number of books together. Their *History of Trade Unionism* was followed by a series of volumes on local government which took them nearly thirty years to complete. They made long journeys to study the politics of the United States, Australia and the Far East, and when they were over seventy they went to Russia to do research for the last of the books they wrote together.

To some people the Webbs were figures of fun and obvious subjects for caricature. H.G. Wells, for instance, parodied them in his novel, *The New Machiavelli*. Others disliked them for their political beliefs and their sometimes devious manoeuvres to implement their policies. And their humourless dedication was often a source of difficulty in personal relationships. Their admirers, however, held them in awesome respect, and many young people, to whom the Webbs were unfailingly encouraging, fell under their influence.

Sidney's love for Beatrice never faltered and he always blessed his good fortune in marrying her. 'As I walked home my eye caught the Evening Star – Venus,' he wrote in one of the daily letters he sent Beatrice when they were apart, 'and I thought of the last time I noticed it in connection with you, on my Oberammergau trip in August 1890, when I wrote to you about it, $30\frac{1}{2}$ years ago! I think it has been a beneficent star.'

Beatrice did not regret the decision she had found so hard to make. There were times, it is true, when she felt sorry that they had married so late and agreed to remain childless in order to devote their lives to public service. Yet she was a loyal and unexpectedly happy partner. 'A marriage of true comradeship makes life in this world one long delight,' she wrote ten years afterwards, 'the sort of happiness which I, at least, never believed possible in those dull, grey days of youth.' She never ceased to be grateful to the man who had unfailingly supported her in times of success and moods of despair. 'If it were not for my beloved partner I should be glad to quit life,' she wrote shortly before she died. 'We have lived the life we liked and done the work we intended to do. What more can a mortal want?...'

Beatrice died in 1943 and Sidney in 1947. Their ashes were buried in Westminster Abbey.

Index

Adams, Annie, 66
Argoed, The, 12, 19, 22, 41, 48, 53, 57, 58

Barnett, Henrietta and Samuel, 18, 29, 49
Bland, Hubert, 66
Booth, Charles: background and ideas, 16; plans social survey, 32, 40; invites Beatrice to join Board of Statistical Research, 40; works with B., 44–5, 51–3, 54; Chamberlain's reaction to his paper, 47; Booth Survey, 57, 61; and British Association, 93
Booth, Charles and Mary: friendship with Beatrice, 16–17, 32, 43, 49; intellectual influence on B., 17, 45, 69; and Sidney Webb, 69, 105–6; estrangement from B., 123–4, 129; reconciliation with B., 135, 140
Booth, Mary: and Beatrice, 16, 31–3, 39, 44, 57–8
Brigden, Clara, 122
Bright, John, 26

Browning, Robert, 59, 96
Burns, John, 58

Chamberlain, Arthur, 47
Chamberlain, Austen, 20
Chamberlain, Beatrice, 20, 21, 26, 42
Chamberlain, Clara, see Ryland
Chamberlain, Joseph: personal and political background, 20–1; early meetings with Beatrice, 21–5; political career, 26, 33, 36–7, 53; and B., 27–8, 30–3, 36–9, 46–8; and unemployment, 36–7; and Home Rule, 39, 47; resignation from Liberal Party, 39; estrangement from B., 48–9, 77, 99; marriage, 53, 54–5, 107; see also Charles Booth, Kate Courtney, Theresa Cripps, Beatrice Potter
Charity Organisation Society, 18, 22
Chevalier, Michel, 5
Contemporary Review, 73
Co-operative movement, 23, 54,

144